RUTH RENDELL'S SUFFOLK

RUTH RENDELL'S SUFFOLK

—◆●◆—

PHOTOGRAPHS BY
PAUL BOWDEN

HUTCHINSON

LONDON

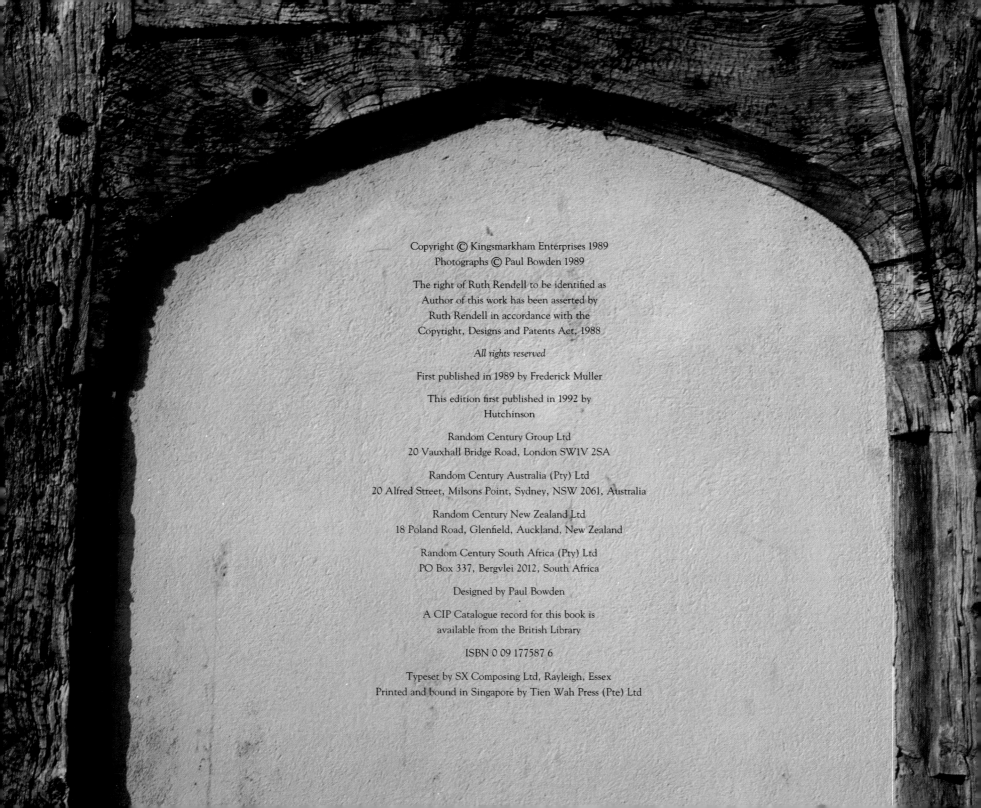

First published in 1989 by Frederick Muller

This edition first published in 1992 by
Hutchinson

Random Century Group Ltd
20 Vauxhall Bridge Road, London SW1V 2SA

Random Century Australia (Pty) Ltd
20 Alfred Street, Milsons Point, Sydney, NSW 2061, Australia

Random Century New Zealand Ltd
18 Poland Road, Glenfield, Auckland, New Zealand

Random Century South Africa (Pty) Ltd
PO Box 337, Bergvlei 2012, South Africa

Designed by Paul Bowden

A CIP Catalogue record for this book is
available from the British Library

ISBN 0 09 177587 6

Typeset by SX Composing Ltd, Rayleigh, Essex
Printed and bound in Singapore by Tien Wah Press (Pte) Ltd

For their generous help and co-operation in making this book possible, my thanks are due to the following:

Maureen Baker-Munton, Monty Baker-Munton, Sam Block, Douglas Brown, Pat Brown, Elizabeth Burton, Josie Foden, John Hayward, Marilyn Hayward, Perdita Hunt, Heather Hyne, Reggie Hyne, P. D. James, Charmaine Keep, Jonathan Keep, Denny Richardson, Donald Simpson, Richard Titford, Sarah Titford, Jeanne Wayre, Philip Wayre, Deirdre Wollaston and Nicholas Wollaston.

To them this book is dedicated.

Sunrise (page 1)

Suffolk sky
(previous page)

Gifford's Hall (opposite)

ALSO BY RUTH RENDELL

To Fear a Painted Devil
Vanity Dies Hard
The Secret House of Death
One Across, Two Down
The Face of Trespass
A Demon in My View
A Judgement in Stone
Make Death Love Me
The Lake of Darkness
Master of the Moor
The Killing Doll
The Tree of Hands
Live Flesh
Talking to Strange Men
The Bridesmaid

Chief Inspector Wexford novels
From Doon with Death
A New Lease of Death
Wolf to the Slaughter
The Best Man to Die
Some Lie and Some Die

Shake Hands for Ever
A Sleeping Life
Put On by Cunning
The Speaker of Mandarin
An Unkindness of Ravens
The Veiled One

Short Stories
The Fallen Curtain
Means of Evil
The Fever Tree
The New Girl Friend

Omnibuses
Collected Short Stories
Wexford: An Omnibus
The Second Wexford
  Omnibus

Novella
Heartstones

Inside Edwardstone
Church

A house in Lady Street,
Lavenham (opposite)

CONTENTS

———▸●◂———

INTRODUCTION.. 14

TOWERS OF GOLD.. 17

HEAVEN OR NEAR IT.. 27

THE RIVER BANK.. 34

HIGHLANDS... 41

PERSIAN ROSES.. 49

AN ANTIQUARY AND ANCIENT PLACES............. 54

PLOVERS IN THE BORDER COUNTRY.................. 60

ALL THAT LIES ON THE BANKS OF THE STOUR...... 68

THE MOLECATCHER'S DAUGHTER...................... 74

GHOSTS AND ANGLO-SAXON PENNIES................ 80

FULL AND FAIR ONES, COME AND BUY................ 84

GREEN VISITORS... 87

CASTLINGS HALL.. 93

SPIRELET.. 96

A GENTLE HOUSE... 100

THE ESTUARY OF THE ALDE............................... 104

SHOP WINDOW.. 112

SNAPE... 117

THE MALT HOUSE.. 120

THE EXTENDED VALLEY..................................... 122

FOUR LIONS AND FOUR WILD MEN..................... 128

LOST CITY.. 134

LOST, UTTERLY LOST AND FORLORN................... 136

INDEX.. 142

On the Green at Hartest

Gargoyle at Stoke-by-Nayland (overleaf)

INTRODUCTION

—▶●◀—

Suffolk is not my native place. It is mine only by adoption. I have no roots here, no ancestors' bones lying in Suffolk churchyards, and I chose to live here for unromantic and prudent reasons.

When I was young my earliest love was Devon. Someone told me you could buy a cottage on the edge of Dartmoor for fifty pounds. This may have been true. In any case it was hard for me to imagine how I should get so vast a sum together. I mourned the south-west without giving up hope of it, rather in the way the Derry Air lyricist bids the years fly faster that he may sooner see the vale beloved so well.

The cottage I came to own in Suffolk had been sold as part of a job lot at about the same time as I was dreaming of my Dartmoor home. The price for this whole clutch of houses was a few hundred pounds. Later on, when it became mine, its value had increased into the low thousands – the very low thousands – and the villagers were shaking their heads over the profligacy of London weekenders.

Polstead is the village where Corder murdered or may not have murdered Maria Marten in the Red Barn. A surprising number of people think this is the reason for my living there. I will not say Maria Marten was unknown to me before I came to Polstead, but I knew of her only as the ill-fated heroine of the most popular of Victorian melodramas, not who she had been or where she came from. Polstead was chosen because it is only 65 miles from London. It is nevertheless in deep pastoral countryside, and driving to it in the early seventies when my father was still alive took me past his door and made Friday night or Sunday afternoon visits easy.

It was in Suffolk then and it is in Suffolk now. Country boundaries used to be judged by the location and name of the authority to which one paid rates. Today it is the Post Office which makes the rules. Since Colchester is in Essex and Colchester is decreed as our postal district, we feel as if bureaucratically transplanted five miles over the boundary. Some of my neighbours, with creaking contrivance, require themselves to be addressed as living at Polstead, Suffolk, via Colchester. At present I am bowing to the Post Office. Why not? Some of the loveliest country in England, Constable's Country, is on the other side of the Stour.

I moved out of my pretty thatched cottage six years ago. Coming to this house on the northern bank of the River Box, I ceased to be a weekender and became a Suffolk dweller with a vote in the constituency of South Suffolk, a little wood of my own and eleven and a half acres of Suffolk earth. And began to take a serious look at this county which had become, and probably will always be, my home.

*

It is not a county of features. There are no rushing streams, no broad sheets of water, no cliff-girt seashore, no downs, no picturesque rock outcroppings. It was Ruskin who said that

Rocks of wood
(previous page)

14

'mountains are the beginning and the end of all scenery,' so we may wonder what he would have made of Suffolk where there are scarcely hills of any height and the highest ground is not much over 400 feet above sea level.

Ours is a man-made scenery. Even our lakes and our blue-clay ponds man has made for his vistas and for his horses. Hedges were planted, hedges were removed and now they are being put back again. Screens of elms, without which some of our poets could hardly have imagined their England, have disappeared from our landscape. The glory of East Anglia is in its churches and its domestic architecture. It is true to say that though it may have been surrounded by estates of modern houses or, worse from an aesthetic point of view, by industrial complexes, you will not find a village in Suffolk that is not pretty. You will hardly find an ugly church or a mean village street.

The farmer may have put up silos that look like something on a rocket testing station but his house remains gracious. 'Infilling' in the villages, a sprawling bus garage or car park, has left untouched those quiet corners where pink plaster contrasts with flintwork and an open door offers a glimpse of a garden of daffodils under a mulberry tree. And the best churches in England are here, a statement that readers may dispute, though not I think very effectively. The biggest are here and the tiniest, the oldest, the rich woolmen's pride with the richest furnishing.

Suffolk's rivers have the loveliest names in England. If you read them in a novel with a setting invented by the author you would shake your head in disbelief. All this is too romantic, too prettily charming to be true. But the Lark and the Linnet, the Dove and the Bat, the Gleme and the Blyth are all real.

I have not chosen to write about Lavenham or Bury St Edmund's, Long Melford or Clare. Others have done this for me, perhaps done it better than I could, certainly with more

knowledge. Those are the tourist centres, not touristy as my once loved West Country has become, but popular enough, names that strangers to Suffolk know, places thoroughly photographed for the guidebooks. I have tried instead to bring to my readers' notice certain corners of this county they might otherwise have rushed past on their journeys to Lavenham and Bury and Lowestoft. I have tried to show them houses they may very likely never see because they will never find them, but which will give them an idea of what treasures Suffolk has. The exceptions are Aldeburgh and Snape. They could not have been left out.

Like the young man of Bay Shore (When his girl friend said, I adore/The beautiful sea/Replied, I agree/It's pretty but what is it for?) I am not fond of the seaside. But ours is the least spoilt of English coastlines and no book about Suffolk would be about Suffolk without something more than a hint in it that the sea is there. In the past, it was an encroaching threatening dragon which left little doubt as to what it was for. It was a sea monster devouring the low cliffs of soft brown sand, the farmers' fields and at Dunwich a whole thriving populous city. And it is still unconquered.

Nor could any book be contemplated today with an area of south-east England as its subject and leave out the storm of October 16, 1987, the great gale which we all learned to call The Hurricane. We have been told that this wind destroyed fifteen million trees in the south-eastern counties. It made its way in a broad sweep, with the swing of a giant scythe, from the coast of Hampshire up through Sussex and Kent, bypassing with the worst of its fury a corner of Essex, and spending its force on Suffolk until it disappeared into the North Sea.

The whole face of southern England would be changed by the devastation the hurricane caused, we were told at the time, and the implication was that it would be changed for the worse. In Suffolk, at least, this seems not to have been so. A year of exceptional regeneration has followed. In places where fine trees fell, hitherto unseen views have opened out. Light let into woodland for the first time in a century has killed stinging nettles and encouraged the growth of aconites and wood anemones, meadowsweet and campion, wild garlic and monkshood. One of the acts of the storm was to destroy the poplar plantations. A Dedham Vale conservationist told us that the countryside now looks much more as it did in Constable's day before matchstick poplars were grown as a crop.

But thousands of tall and ancient trees went down. Until they were gone we had no idea our wood contained the finest stand of ash in South Suffolk. None of us would have believed a mere wind could pierce a wood and spiral in the heart of it like a tornado, wrenching three hundred-year-old oaks out of the ground as easily as the gardener's hand pulls out weeds. It was the handsomest, tallest, oldest trees that went. If 'their departure is taken for misery and their going from us to be utter destruction', and we shall never see their replacements attain any size in our lifetime, at least we have replaced them and have wood enough to build a village of timber-framed houses furnished in old English oak.

The photographs in this book might have been different if the storm had never happened or had come a week later when less foliage was on the trees to help the wind overturn them. It may no longer be true that there are fewer forests and more trees in England than any other European country. The appearance of some of the houses and churches I have written about has been changed by the loss of oak and ash and some of the rare ornamentals which were features of gardens. Villages have become a little more stark and panoramas of meadows and copses bleaker. There will be pictures my readers will look at, just as there must be visitors to Suffolk who look at the land itself, and wonder at certain imbalances and asymmetries, at limbs inexplicably lopped and woodland clumsily thinned. I ask them to remember the hurricane and to make allowances. Time will heal the woods. At least the hurricane and the consequent loss of trees has brought about a re-planting on a generous and unprecedented scale.

If there is more here about South Suffolk and the Stour Valley than the rest of the county, it is because these places are more immediately familiar to me. They are home. But I have gone north and west as well and to the sea.

I have made no concessions at all to what people may want but have chosen exclusively the places and things that I like. Here and there I have mentioned things I particularly dislike. In one case I have unashamedly written about a friend's house, my excuse being that it is worth writing about. Suffolk is full of ghosts and there are two or three here.

Because I did not want to produce a guide or a brochure of tourism, I have written not only about my favourite places but also about two of my favourite societies. And because I am a reader and one of those who, without knowing anything about painting or music, knows what she likes, I have written something about our musicians and our writers and painters. I have used the experiences of my friends and neighbours and the stories they have told me. And as a writer of suspenseful fiction, I have naturally tried to solve a mystery or two.

Silhouette at Bures

The broken horizon
(overleaf)

TOWERS OF GOLD

—➤●◄—

The church at Stoke-by-Nayland has a 'great red tower' which they say can be seen from Harwich, 20 miles off. It is only red as the Maria Marten Red Barn in Polstead was, in certain lights and at certain times. Constable was always painting it and not above moving it to other parts of the Stour Valley to suit his purposes.

A Lord Mayor of London at the beginning of the 16th century, Sir William Capel, was born in Stoke. He had a great devotion to Henry VII and once dissolved a pearl in wine to drink to the King's health. Another time he entertained the King at a banquet, lit a fire and burned in it the bonds given him for money Henry had borrowed. The Maltings and the Guildhall in School Street, are the finest village houses. For some reason, round here they are always just known as 'the weavers'. All that survives of Sir John Soane's Tendring Hall is a deep-eaved pavilion, painted yellow and white, and apparently designed as a fishing lodge. People hereabouts call it The Temple. The bit of road where it stands is known as the Nayland Straight. When you get your first real motorbike you prove yourself by doing a ton along there.

A certain Lady Ann Windsor's tomb is in the church, with alabaster effigy and alabaster children at her head and feet. Round about the time, early in the 17th century, when she was founding a hospital here for the poor women of Stoke, a house was being rebuilt down at Thorington Street. There are two Thoringtons in Suffolk, one up in the north-east near Blythburgh, the other within Stoke parish, a backwater with a palace in it, a jewel in a rustic setting.

This is a house I should like to own but never shall. There would have to be an Act of Parliament before Thorington Hall could be sold. Since the early 1940s it has been in the possession of the National Trust who describe it as 'one of the largest and most beautiful of Suffolk's timber-framed farmhouses'.

To call Thorington a farmhouse seems mildly shocking. The Umfreville family who occupied it for some of its long life must have been grand farmers. The house we see today is very largely the product of the massive rebuilding between 1620 and 1630 which increased its size threefold. A high brick wall bounds the front garden and its pair of weeping ash trees. This wall was built about seventy years later and the gate is a rare survival from that time. As you approach from the Stoke-by-Nayland side the wall is the first thing you see, and then, enough to make the unwary motorist swerve and swoop into the ditch, the glorious house elevates itself before the eye in peaks and towers of gold.

Not gold, of course, and only one tower, built to house the newel stair. But the effect, dreamlike and deceptive, is of height emerging from misty depths and of many steep gables. The colour which the National Trust painted it after the restructuring and re-plastering of the walls, a warm ochreish yellow, is that of sunlight on cherrywood or of a very ripe mira-

Thorington Hall

belle plum. Out of the roof rises a six-stacked cluster chimney with star-shaped caps from which protrude spikes curved and knobbed, like the horns of a snail.

Beautiful fireplaces, of stone, of oak with inset Georgian grate, one inlaid with Dutch tiles of Biblical scenes, not white with blue but white with a curious unexpected mauve, have shafts leading up to the various chimneys. They are usable by those with the strength and patience to carry logs and coal. There is no central heating and the house is large. In winter, and winters are hard in Suffolk, every water pipe going in and every waste pipe leading out freezes.

'The cold is quite funny,' says Deirdre Wollaston. 'One night in bed I said to Nick, "It's snowing on us." It seemed unbelievable but sure enough we found snow on the bedside table.'

The snow infiltrates the windows, pours down the chimneys. With a kind of cheerful resignation the Wollastons remark that it is 'very uncomfortably cold here in winter.'

They have never seen the ghost of Thorington Hall.

'We had a guest who woke up in the night and felt the presence of a young woman in the room with her. She wasn't frightened, it didn't seem threatening.'

The ghost is the Brown Lady. She walks a passage in the eastern range of the building, or that at any rate is where she was seen by a previous occupant. Fred and Elizabeth Burton came to Thorington Hall just before the Second World War and remained as caretakers when the Penroses moved to Canada.

'We used to hear the footsteps when we were in bed at night,' says Mrs Burton. 'I was very frightened the first time it happened. My husband went to see what it was and I thought he'd never come back.'

They got used to the footsteps. They accepted that these were harmless sounds they were to hear from time to time. His widow believes Fred Burton was psychic and that this may account for the ghostly woman manifesting herself to him. It was during the war and Mrs Burton had gone to Leeds to a wedding.

'He went upstairs to see to the blackout. It was a summer evening and he was alone in the house with our dogs. At the top of the stairs he saw this person in a brown habit. He thought it must be a friend of mine and then he realised she was wearing this old-fashioned dress. He looked at her and she put her hand up to her mouth as if to show she shouldn't be there and she vanished through the white wall.

'He wasn't a man who was easily frightened but that frightened him. He phoned me and asked me to come home. He said, "Bess, I'll be glad when you're back." It wasn't till I was home that he told me what he'd seen.

'That was the only time he ever saw anything, and we never heard the footsteps after that. But an odd thing happened. We had this dog who used to jump up at people. One day my husband found him on the landing jumping up at someone and wagging his tail – only there was nobody there.'

The River Box, a tributary of the Stour which it joins at Boxted Cross not far from here, flows south within thirty yards of Thorington Hall. The house is by far the most conspicuous feature of this tiny settlement. Curiously, White's Suffolk of 1844 includes no occupants of this lovely house in its list of Stoke residents, though a Mrs Mary Leving was at Thorington Cottage and William Scowen kept the Rose Inn.

Did it stand empty and decaying, abandoned to the melancholy tenancy of the Brown Lady?

The back of the house is no less lovely but it is quite different. Here a grave and austere Jacobean house observes its gardens and the valley of the River Box beyond. It is hard to believe, standing on the lawn and looking at mullioned windows and smooth golden walls, that the house could have

Window at Thorington

The Newel Stair

Inside window at
Thorington Hall
(opposite)

24

undergone the slightest change since its creation in the reign of Charles I. But photographs from 1910 show it semi-derelict, ivy-hung, 'Georgianised', particularly in the matter of windows. It was four years later that it ceased to be a permanent home and its land was incorporated in the estate of the Rowley family. The house fell into utter dereliction. Between the two world wars, up until the middle thirties, there were successive proposals to demolish it.

While rejoicing in the rescue of Thorington Hall, it is difficult not to reflect on those houses, approaching it certainly in loveliness, which were not so fortunate. Thorington Hall's multi-flight staircase of glowing grey oak might have been lost, and with it the newel posts carved severally with open hearts, with lozenges, roses, sunflowers and tulips. Also cast into the demolition men's rubble heaps might have been the window catches, wrought iron of the 17th century, which still perform their function better than those installed fifty years ago.

The rescue of Thorington Hall was largely due to the intervention of Lionel Penrose, who bought it, reputedly for £700, in 1935. Penrose, doctor of medicine and geneticist, put the restoration into the hands of the pastiche architect Marshall Sisson. War came two years afterwards and in 1941 Thorington Hall was made over to the National Trust with the proviso that Lionel Penrose should enjoy a lifelong tenancy.

The present tenant, with a twenty-one year lease more than half gone, is novelist, journalist and critic Nicholas Wollaston who came to live there 'in the golden summer of 1975'. He and his wife Deirdre, who at the time had a five-floor Georgian house in Islington, first came to view the Hall in February, found it gloomy and forbidding, said, 'Not for us.' But they returned in the spring and that was enough.

The National Trust had toyed with the idea of turning it into a museum. Among other uses it was to be a gallery for Constable paintings, here in the heart of the Constable country. There were rumours that someone proposed a restaurant here, another an antique shop. It became instead a family house for the Wollastons and their three children, Sophy, Sam and Josh.

Deirdre Wollaston, an art historian, worked on the floors herself, restoring them and exposing the pale gleaming wood which lay beneath a hard black crust of paint and polish and stain. She worked, by hand and without a sander for fear of causing damage, on the main or 'new' staircase, removing paint from the oak newels and balusters. The house is deeply loved by her and her husband, who enjoy it as perhaps few people enjoy the appearance and fabric and distinction of their homes.

'It's a wonderful house to have a lot of people in,' she says.

They have had music weeks with an orchestra playing in the drawing room. Sophy had a party with a disco in the curious subterranean room, half cellar, half kitchen, where above the brickwork base you can see the lath and plaster composition of the walls. Even on a warm day it is cold down there. In January and February the iciness of Thorington Hall is ferocious.

HEAVEN OR NEAR IT

Whenever I go to America people apologise to me for things not being old enough. I try to reassure them. Age, after all, equals beauty only in architecture and perhaps furniture, and not then in everyone's eyes. But they persist in explaining to me that a house built in 1890 really is old to them because these things are relative, and so on, and I smile and agree.

England, in their imagination and their experience, is a treasure house full of ancient artefacts – and the museum itself is immeasurably old. Who is to say they are wrong? A great deal of it is like that, only we don't notice because we are used to it. Among the places essential for American tourists to visit is Groton where most people (including M. R. James) think John Winthrop, first governor of Massachusetts Bay Colony, was born in 1588, confusing him with his son and namesake. I hope they are not told so by the guide on their coach tour.

Edwardstone was the birthplace of John Winthrop the Elder. Twice he came back to England which must have been a rather more daunting adventure in the middle of the 17th century. Americans may regard him as a founding father but I suppose he saw himself as a colonist only. There are places called after Winthrop on both sides of the Atlantic, a Boxford in New England and a Groton where the school is, but no Edwardstone.

Winthrop was a country squire who had emigrated on account of his dissatisfaction with Charles I's anti-puritan policies. This was puritan country. A builder I know, restoring a house in Boxford nearby, found a 17th century high-crown hat up a chimney. Some time during the centuries it must have fallen out of the back of a cupboard. All he found in my chimney was birds' nests and soot and the brick footholds the sweepers' boys used when they climbed up.

Edwardstone is not really far from Sudbury or Lavenham but it seems to be in the middle of nowhere. The church of St Mary the Virgin is one of those which stand in a manorial park. Edwardstone Hall has gone but its park is still lovely, with long quiet views across the distant meadows.

A red brick archway with lodge attached stands at the entrance to the park and church. Known hereabouts as Temple Bar, it was built about 1840 and is believed to have been modelled on the original Temple Bar in London, now re-erected in Hertfordshire. It doesn't look much like that to me. There was once an avenue of elms leading down to Temple Bar, but they went the way of all our elms. Chestnuts have been planted to replace them.

In his book on Suffolk churches, which is as a bible, Munro Cautley calls St Mary's 'fine' but goes on to dismiss it as containing nothing of interest, 'except perhaps the brass to Benjamin and Elizabeth Brand dated 1620. . .' This brass is on the floor in the north-east corner near the organ. The crests of the man and woman it commemorates are there and so is their huge family, a queue of cloaked sons and another of mantled daughters, father and mother in their ruffs and stiff ornate gowns.

The inscription reads (in language somewhat up-dated): 'To the precious memory of Benjamin Brand of Edwardstone Hall Esquire and Elizabeth his wife whom, when Providence after 35 years divided, death, after 12 days divorcement, re-united; who leaving their rare examples to six sons and six daughters (all nursed with her un-borrowed milk) blessed with poor men's prayers, embalmed with numerous tears, lie here reposed.' An improvement, surely, on the Clopton epitaph.

Nothing of interest? Quaint treasures include a corkscrew, with a little brush incorporated into its handle, for drawing the corks of Communion wine bottles and cleaning their tops. There are thin Roman bricks worked into the south wall of the chancel. The organ is odd for a small country church. Encased in crimson, studded with the gilded suns that gleam star-like every-where in this church, it contains part of an organ built by Father Smith in 1670 for the Sheldonian Theatre in Oxford and is said to be the oldest Father Smith machine in the country.

The octagonal Stuart pulpit has an octagonal tester over it which actually works. If the preacher leans beyond its limits his voice disappears. The best way to appreciate the rather unusual King post roof, the vicar says, is by lying on a pew looking upwards with your head as near the centre of the roof line as possible. There are more suns with curly golden rays up there on the timbers. The reredos behind the altar depicts Calvary and a skull lies on the ground at the foot of the cross.

Nine chandeliers once held 96 candles. They must have been a marvellous sight. In 1957, when electricity came, they were modified to use light bulbs. The chandeliers are wrought iron, made by a Northamptonshire blacksmith, and the big one in the chancel is entwined with oak and maple leaves in gilt and unidentifiable red-eyed flowers. The chancel roof is a

Altar piece

pale bluish-green, a bird's egg green, with crimson hatchings and more gilt suns, big and small.

St Mary's is 500 years old, a true flint-walled square-towered Suffolk church. If you go in on your own when no one else is there, when no service is in progress, it is not just quiet inside, it is silent. The silence slips over you like a thin clinging cloak as soon as you have closed the door behind you. We are used to silence hereabouts, or what we call silence – quiet that is mostly disturbed or enlivened by the hum of agricultural machinery, birdsong, the lowing of cattle, the trembling buzz of damp in the power lines, distant traffic never ceasing, the everlasting wind rustling. Inside St Mary's is a tranquil time-less silence which reminds the visitor that this is how many places must have been in the Middle Ages when this church was young.

The dead are still buried here. Some of the gravestones are old, half vanished in long grass and wild flowers. One of the three Pryke tombs by the chancel wall gapes as if some product of James's imagination has creaked his way out of it, but the churchyard is wide open to the sunshine and cowslips bloom there in the spring. A notice in the porch tells the visitor that some of the grass is left uncut, the better to help the survival of rarer animals and plants.

'Is this heaven or is it just near it?' someone said to the vicar after a funeral. The most important thing about the church as far as he is concerned is that it is always open, never locked.

'It is defenceless.'

The vicar is Richard Titford who came there with his wife Sarah six years ago. This is a united benefice of three parishes, Groton, Edwardstone and Little Waldingfield.

'But Edwardstone is our parish church. If we end our days here it is in that parish church we shall be buried.'

It was one of many Suffolk churches whose bells were

derelict. The tenor bell had a large piece of its lip missing. Only the treble and fifth could be rung.

'They were just being donged,' Sarah said, 'until we were advised to stop donging in case we caused more damage. Then they were silent.'

Early in 1985 the Parochial Church Council set up its trust to restore the Edwardstone bells. The aim was to have the bells ringing again by Christmas 1986. The entire cost of restoration was to be £24,000 and it was raised in less time than the trust anticipated.

Sarah Titford was the prime mover in the restoration. She had learned to ring three years before when she and her husband lived in Manchester and he was a curate there. The Captain of the Tower told her she was a natural ringer. She succeeded in ringing a peal in method after only eighteen months.

One of the things she did to raise money at Edwardstone was charter Concorde on November 20, St Edmund's Day. It was a gamble which came off. Two years later, on a British Airtours holiday flight to Faro, Richard was reading an article in the in-flight magazine about the uses to which Concorde had been put. He saw their own enterprise mentioned. The man sitting next to him said,

'Some nutty vicar hired it to mend his church bells and they say he's on this flight.'

The list of the bells with their names reads rather like that passage out of Dorothy Sayers' *The Nine Tailors*:

Treble Bell: Founded by John Waylett, of Bishop's Stortford, in 1709, with inscription 'Mr Cook and Nuting. CW 1709.'

Second Bell: Founded by John Waylett, of Bishop's Stortford, in 1710, with inscription 'Tuned by Wm. Culpeck, 1710.'

Third Bell: Founded by Miles Graye II, of Colchester, in 1640, with inscription 'Miles Graye made me. M 1640.'

Fourth Bell: Founded by Miles Graye II, of Colchester, in 1641, with inscription 'Miles Graye made me. 1641.M'

Fifth Bell: Founded by Miles Graye III, of Colchester, in 1663, with inscription 'Miles Graye made me, 1663.'

Tenor Bell: Founded by Thomas Gardiner of Sudbury, about 1712, with inscription:

'About ty second Culpeck is wrett,
Because the founder want dwett.
Their judgements ware but bad at last,
Or else this bell I never had cast.'

The first down was the treble. Four more joined it for despatch to the Loughborough bellfounders. The old tenor was past repair with a piece missing from her soundbow. Most of the old frame was burned in the churchyard and the tower was restored. The front five bells came back in August with new canon-retaining headstocks, with cherry red ironwork and the new Taylor tenor inscribed as the Morden College Bell. Susanna Brand of Edwardstone Hall married John Morden, merchant, of London, in 1662. At the end of that century he founded a college at Blackheath for tradesmen fallen upon hard times, or 'decayed merchants' as they were called in the original charter. Wren designed Morden College and there has been a link between it and Edwardstone since 1700 when it was opened. The emended list of bells now ends with: Tenor Bell, John Taylor of Loughborough, 1986.

For a long time Mrs Cora Green of Edwardstone had donged the bells but the last full-circle ringing had been in 1885. One hundred and one years later a service was held to dedicate the new bells. Sarah Titford was one of the ringers, as she has been ever since whenever the Edwardstone peal is rung. But now she is the Captain of her own tower.

The Brand Brass
(previous page)

The new tenor

33

THE RIVER BANK

The otters leap and dive and swoop for their food. The big ones gobble fish, roll languorously in the water, plunge and embrace, sit up begging, dog-like, whiskery muzzles smiling. They have the deftness and swimming skills of fish in fur coats, the sinuousness of the eels they love to eat, faces as appealing as seals and as sharp as cats.

We might have had the otters in our corner of the county if planning permission had been granted to Philip Wayre. He owned the land at Raydon and struggled for three years to make this the site for his plan to breed otters and reintroduce them to the wild.

His home was in Norfolk at Great Witchingham. He had first become interested in otters when he made a film for Anglia Television called 'Wind in the Reeds' in the early sixties. For about 12 years during the sixties and seventies he presented nearly all Anglia's wildlife programmes.

The film required otter cubs but none was available even at the huge price he was offering of £100 each. Otters had become rare and were a severely endangered species. In the end he had to get his animals from America. But soon he was the only man in Britain breeding the otter in captivity, the first to attempt this since the 1880s.

This was in the sixties, the time of the purge of the coypu, the concerted drive against this South American mammal which had escaped from captivity to find in East Anglian ponds and rivers a congenial habitat. Coypu trappers were also catching otters. Because they could get £5 a pelt they were shooting the otters in cages with .22 rifles. Philip Wayre offered £10 each for living otters and got an immediate response.

Most of the animals brought to him he released into the wild but he kept eight or nine of them and began to breed them. The land at Raydon was sold and about 30 acres was bought along a stretch of the River Waveney where the Otter Trust now is. Philip Wayre, who is Chairman of the Trust, and his wife Jeanne, its Director, made over 23 acres of this land to the Trust at a peppercorn rent, keeping 8 acres for themselves and the house called River Farm where they live.

Earsham is properly just inside Norfolk. But the River Waveney is the natural boundary between the counties, its water surely half Suffolk water. Besides, the Post Office does something similar up there to what it does to us and gives Earsham a Suffolk postal address. That is my excuse for adopting the otters and the Trust into our county, at least for my own purposes here.

The Trust is open to the public from the beginning of April until the end of October and 43,000 people came to see the otters this year. A small side stream is divided into sections for them, a large swimming place for each breeding pair.

'I'm a bit vague about the number,' Philip Wayre says. 'We don't know exactly how many cubs there may be lurking about.'

The river bank

34

You always see the otters when you go to Earsham. I take people who come to stay with me, particularly children. They always ask if they will really see them or if it is a matter of luck or chance. Go at feeding time, noon and four in the afternoon. The noon feed isn't necessary, a measure designed for the visitors' pleasure more than the animals' need. Sea fish bought by the ton on the quay at Lowestoft is what they get, that and a mixture of minced raw beef and canned carnivore diet plus dead day-old chicks from a local hatchery.

Most of the otters are British but some are the Asian short-clawed variety.

'We keep them for the people to see. British otters are shy, solitary, nocturnal, and you can't keep a pair together on view. Asians are social, diurnal, playful, talkative and friendly. Of course it is the British kind we release into the wild.'

Eighteen in all have been set free, a pair recently into a Norfolk river and two more into the River Stour in Dorset. If the release of a captive-bred animal is to succeed, the operation must be scientifically organised. It is not a matter of finding a likely looking river and releasing young otters. At the Trust the young are removed from their mothers at eight to ten months and then put into large semi-natural pre-release enclosures where they stay for six months or more until they are removed to the release site. Although these otters are fed daily they are not otherwise disturbed and are rarely seen. It is vital that they should neither be tame nor accustomed to human beings.

Or so Philip Wayre believed. 'We had an otter called Riddle, a breeding female. She was used to us, used to people, a tame otter bred here. One of our staff left the gate to her pen open and she disappeared. We thought we had lost her. Then quite a long while later when we thought she must have settled in the wild someone saw some otter droppings outside the gate. I set a trap but without success. I tried another way. The otter dens are wooden, about two feet square, with tunnels attached to keep out draughts. I put Riddle's den outside with some good fresh bedding in it. Next morning there she was inside, lying there curled up asleep. That made me think again about otters accustoming themselves to the wild, about how any otter, however used to people, seemed to adapt to the wild. But I knew she must be happy here to come home like that.'

They look sweet; they are red in tooth and claw. I once thought of having a pair of otters. After all, I have a large deep pond, almost a lake, which is full of fish, hundreds upon hundreds of red-finned rudd which the Tendring Hall herons come fishing for. The otters, I learned, would clear the pond of fish, basely desert me and move on. They are rapacious fishermen, hungry hunters. An alighting bird they will have, a seagull, a duck, a swan even.

'Trout may get away,' says Philip Wayre. 'But most fish are stupid. They try to escape by hiding themselves in the weed but they leave their tails poking out and the otter gets them.'

Besides the otters, there are muntjack deer which gambol about unhindered. They, or their ancestors, came originally from India by way of Woburn. Hosts of wildfowl are to be seen at Earsham, flying in dense formation or grazing on the green water meadows. You can see wild widgeon grazing twenty yards from the Wayres' house. There are barnacle geese and swan geese, red-breasted geese and teal, scaup and gadwall, pintails and tufted ducks. The red-crested pochard have plump downy heads the colour of polished copper.

'We don't pinion our wildfowl so we can only keep British. They're free, they can leave if they want to, but they don't want to.'

Otters at Earsham

37

Lesser white-fronted geese and western bean geese are bred here and pairs sent back to Sweden to be re-established in Swedish Lapland where their numbers have decreased due to the disturbance of tundra. At Witchingham eagle owls were bred for reintroduction to Sweden and Germany where the species is very threatened. Philip Wayre had an eagle owl called Bubo which was given to him by the Director of the Helsinki zoo. Bubo lived to be 33, used to sit on its block beside its owner on all his television programmes.

It was Philip Wayre who first coined the term 'wildlife park' back in the sixties. He and his wife still have their reserve at Witchingham and the Otter Trust has another in Cornwall. Three wildlife wetland reserves are not open to the public. One is at Swangey Fen on the Upper Thet in Norfolk, another on the River Inny in Cornwall. The third is nearest to home in Suffolk at Stanley Carrs near Beccles.

There are 43 acres of alder swamp, unspoilt, untouched wild land the plough has never disturbed and where the forest is prevented from encroaching. It is fenland where ducks live and sparrowhawks – and the odd otter.

England should be full of such sanctuaries. It seems we can't be trusted to watch over our own countryside, to tread softly, not to plunder or ruin ancient habitats. But it is possible to imagine a new world where 'wild' means cared-for and 're-serve' is just a place as nature made it.

Prancing otter

The white swan
(opposite)

HIGHLANDS

→•←

The skies in Suffolk are bigger than elsewhere. Or so it seems. The explanation can't quite be that this is because the land is flat. In the south where I live and in the Hundred of Risbridge to the west of Bury are rolling hills crowned with woodland. For some other mysterious reason, you can always see a long way in Suffolk and you are always aware of an encircling horizon.

Sometimes in winter the overcast begins to roll back in the middle of the morning. It lifts like a blind drawn up and underneath is a pale blue sky, clear as glass and with a greenish cast to it. The sun hangs low and throws long tree shadows across the huge hedgeless meadows.

The road from Long Melford going north by way of Glemsford passes through what a friend of mine calls bow and arrow country. It is rare in Suffolk to travel far without seeing a house but miles are empty here. You have the feeling that at any time you might come upon Guthrum the Dane and his men on the march or see St Edmund leaning on his spear. Glemsford church stands high on the hill, crowning a ridge, a white-speckled field hanging apron-like below it. At first you take the white for sheep but these are gravestones in a hillside churchyard.

As you climb the winding road, spectacular Monk's Hall stares down at you, a dramatic pink and red house, half-timbered, looking bigger from a distance than when you are under its gables. There is an early 19th century silk mill in Glemsford which once employed 500 people.

On to Boxted and Hawkedon, the road looping and twisting and dropping down into the valley of the Gleme, tall crack willows here and willow saplings with thin red branches. The nut and sloe hedges are thick and high. Hawkedon church stands on a bare green, a lovely church with a brick-topped porch and trefoil frieze. No part of the county is more beautiful than that which lies between Hawkedon and Wickhambrook. It is hilly, lightly wooded, the copper-leaved oaks gathered in copses full of copper-coloured pheasants. By November berries on the holly are red and the hedges red with rose hips. The oak leaves seem to turn a richer bronze up here than in my part of the county where they fade to a soft gold. The last time I was there, a big black cat was hunting in one of these copses, watched by five magpies from the safety of the trees.

There are two houses in Suffolk called Gifford's Hall, both fabulously beautiful. The visitor is prepared by a signpost for the house at Wickhambrook but nothing really prepares you. Trees shelter the mansion. As you approach they seem to part like stage curtains to show the towering gable, the timbering, the five-light and seven-light windows, the tall cluster chimneys. Gifford's Hall has been much restored. A man called Heigham built the original house just over 500 years ago. One of his descendants, Thomas Heigham, lies in the church in effigy of alabaster. He is dressed in armour, his hand on his sword, a 'worthy and well-deserving souldier'.

Suffolk gave so many of its men to the armed forces. Every

High ground

41

Fabulous beast
Gifford's Hall (opposite)

church and churchyard shows its sad commemorations. The men of the Suffolk Volunteer Rifle Corps first made their appearance, in grey uniform and shako, at Bury St Edmunds in June 1861.

The riflemen are coming
From Hadleigh and from Eye,
From Sudbury and Mildenhall,
From places far and nigh,
Stowmarket, Brandon, Wickhambrook,
Brave hearts and true draw near,
Ring out, ring out, blithe Bury bells,
And greet each volunteer.

Along the A road to Bury it is bleaker, open to the winds, but still a glorious countryside. In the midst of this beauty, at Chedburgh, stands the ugliest industrial estate in the county, a hideous pandemonium of grim grey factories, cuboid, funnelled, with steel cylinders and barleysugar aluminium chimneys, visible for miles. It would be. This is the highest part of Suffolk, with Rede on the nearest we have to a mountain only a mile or two away.

Again, it is a matter of looking the other way and pretending the satanic mills aren't there. The way to Whepstead goes past Doveden Hall, a 16th century house with unusual octagonal chimneys. Nearby, in front of the Ark House, is the finest cypress hedge I have ever seen. The only one of its kind I have ever seen, for this is not just Leylandii planted together in a row but sculpted cypresses, trimmed to look like dark green watered silk, flanking a wall topped by stone balls. The garden behind has yellow crab apples and winter flowering trees.

On one side of the road at Whepstead is the new graveyard, on the other the old where ancient illegible gravestones are sunk in the long grass under yews and hollies scarlet with berries. The church is the only one in the country dedicated to St Petronilla, whoever she was, perhaps some Roman virgin martyr.

The part called 'Winter' of his long epic poem *The Seasons*, James Thomson wrote in Stradishall in 1726. Or so they say. Stradishall's church of St Margaret looks transparent on its shallow hilltop in the sunshine, the light streaming through its clerestories.

The village green at Hartest is big and handsome, nearly all the houses which surround it interesting and pretty. White describes Hartest as in 'the bosom of a deep valley'. The river is the Gleme which rises up near Rede and flows into the Stour south of Glemsford. For a change, there are some attractive Victorian buildings here, notably the Boxted and Hartest Club of 1888, as well as a Georgian chapel and a cluster of cottages washed pink and green.

A Hartest house

Houses on the Green at Hartest (overleaf)

PERSIAN ROSES

—▶●◀—

So many of the great houses of the county have disappeared. The middle years of this century saw the demolition of houses at Fornham and Campsey Ash, Thornham Park and Ufford Place, Tendring Hall which Soane designed, and the White House at Bredfield. The Elizabethan High House at Campsey Ash with stepped gables and ornamental chimneys was torn down in 1953. A Tudor mansion at Assington, ancient seat of the Gurdon family, standing in a park with cedars, burned to the ground in 1957. Fire also destroyed Rushbrook Hall, part of which was 13th century, much Tudor, the remainder Georgian.

White's Suffolk, the gazetteer and source book of 1844, while a mine of interesting things, makes grim reading when we come upon the many allusions to demolished buildings. Lines such as 'the remains of it were pulled down' in such and such a year or 'the Priory', 'the Augustinian monastery', 'the Hall' 'were pulled down' are constantly repeated. There was nothing to protect ancient buildings in Georgian and Victorian times – nothing but the whim of a landowner, who might appreciate his Tudor palace or prefer to replace it with what Jane Austen called 'a modern house, new-built'.

Wanton destruction of valuable old houses is now prohibited and their protection a statutory duty. All buildings before 1700 which survive more or less intact must be listed, and many of those built between 1700 and 1840. Such a house, demolished in the 1950s, might have been Boulge Hall, a Queen Anne Mansion, home of the Irish family of Fitzgerald.

George Crabbe, son and namesake of the poet, was Vicar of nearby Bredfield. He built a new house for himself in his parish and it cost him £1,400, a sizeable sum in 1836. Crabbe wrote facetious doggerel – his father's genius was not inherited – and the lines he sent to Fitzgerald, accepting an invitation to dine, end with the words, 'Boulge is my heaven!'

This village, whose name sounds as if it were in some unvisited corner of France, was less than heavenly to Edward Fitzgerald who called it one of the dullest and ugliest places in England. It is hard to understand what he meant. Boulge and its environs today are a beautiful pastoral countryside, thickly wooded, serene in sunshine, bleak and wild in winter. To find his grave, the seeker after literary memorabilia must traverse lanes that are still sandy tracks unchanged surely for a hundred years. Sequestered paths lead through the beechwoods of the park up to the pretty wrought iron gates of the churchyard. The small Norman church, insensitively rebuilt by another Fitzgerald, is St Michael and All Angels, too dark inside to see much and rather gloomy. It might justly be said to be miles from anywhere. The silence is deep, broken only by birdsong.

Perhaps we should remember, however, that Fitzgerald also defended Suffolk when others slighted it.

'What little wind there was,' he wrote, 'carried to us the murmurs of the waves circulating round these coasts so far over a flat country. But people here think that this sound so

St Michael's, Boulge

heard is not from the waves that break, but a kind of prophetic voice from the body of the sea itself announcing great gales. Sure enough, we have got them, however heralded. Now, I say that all this shows that we in this Suffolk are not so completely given over to prose and turnips as some would have us. I have always said that being near the sea, and being able to catch a glimpse of it from the tops of hills and of houses, redeemed Suffolk from dullness; and, at all events, that our turnip-fields, dull in themselves, were at least set all round with an undeniable poetic element.'

Apart from brief excursions to France and London, Fitzgerald never left Suffolk in all his 74 years. He was born in 1809 at Bredfield House and lived for most of his life in a cottage at the bottom of the drive on the estate at Boulge Hall. Here came to visit him the 'Wits of Woodbridge'. Thackeray and Tennyson were his friends and Tennyson wrote, in dedicating a poem to him, that he recalled 'gracious times':

'When in our younger London days,
You found some merit in my rhymes,
And I more pleasure in your praise.'

Fitzgerald is buried in Boulge churchyard near the foot of the tower. His family mausoleum is nearby, a hideous and sinister mock-Gothic edifice that looks as if it flew here, like the holy house of Loreto, from Kensal Green on the look-out for prettier surroundings. By contrast the poet's grave is a plain stone sarcophagus with on one side his name and dates: Edward Fitzgerald, 1809 – 1883, and on the other, by his own choice, 'It is He that hath made us and not we ourselves.' The visitor who does not know would pass it by.

There is nothing to show that here lies the man who made the very free and imaginative translation of the Persian poem we know as 'The Rubaiyat of Omar Khayyam'.

Except the roses. In October 1893 a group of Fitzgerald's admirers who called themselves the Omar Khayyam Club planted a rose tree on his grave. It had been raised from seed grown in Kew Gardens, the seed having been brought from a rose growing on Khayyam's own grave in Persia. In 1972 six roses were planted which had been sent from Naishapur to mark the 2,500th year of the Persian Empire.

'I sometimes think that never blows so red,' wrote Fitzgerald or Khayyam,

'The rose, as where some buried Caesar bled.'

Was Hooker still director of Kew when the Khayyam Club's seed germinated? Joseph Dalton Hooker, of the family which was virtually synonymous with English botany for nearly a century, was born in Halesworth up near the Norfolk border in 1817. Hooker, in association with George Bentham, produced a vast work called the 'Genera Plantarum' about world flora which described 7,569 varieties and 97,000 species of seed-bearing plants. His wife was called Hyacinth, which I like to think was the subject of gentle family jokes.

Although he was born in Norfolk, although he roamed Spain and the Celtic lands and London, George Borrow lived in Suffolk longer than he lived anywhere. He had a house at Oulton near Lowestoft, and his study was an octagonal summer house, now gone, on the north-west shore of Oulton Broad, and there he wrote his books. Borrow used to walk about the lanes in a broad-brimmed hat and Spanish cloak. He walked for miles. Once, when he had to go up to London for an interview with the Bible Society, he walked there from Norwich, 112 miles in 27 hours. He walked across Cornwall and the Isle of Man and after his mother's death, found consolation in tremendous walks about the Highlands.

Borrow published 'The Bible in Spain', which sold in large numbers and he became a famous man. The coming of the

'. . . Bury me by some
sweet gardenside.'

railway from Lowestoft to Reedham had driven him out of Suffolk but he came back again later and died there.

He was acquainted with Theodore Watts-Dunton, Algernon Swinburne's friend. Born in Belgravia, growing up in Northumbria and the Isle of Wight, Swinburne often visited the Suffolk coast with Watts-Dunton. He loved the sea. In 'A Literary Pilgrim in England' Edward Thomas describes him as having added Dunwich to the poets' country. Swinburne answers the question: where is man?

> 'Here is all the end of all his glory -
> Just grass and barren silent stones.
> Dead, like him, one hollow tower and hoary
> Naked in the sea-wind stands and moans,
> Filled and thrilled with its perpetual story;
> Here where earth is dense with dead men's bones.'

A forgotten writer of sentimental biography, Agnes Strickland, was admired and popular in her day. In collaboration with her sister she wrote *Lives of the Queens of England*. It is said that when she timidly approached Borrow and offered to present him with the twelve volumes of this work, he shouted at her, 'For God's sake don't, madam. I shouldn't know where to put them or what to do with them.' A member of a literary family, she was born in London but died at Southwold in 1874 before the railway arrived five years later and it became a popular resort. But it remained 'one of the happiest and most picturesque seaside towns in England,' writes Pevsner.

Blundeston, not far from Oulton, a village whose church has a round tower the tallest and thinnest in East Anglia, Dickens made the birthplace of David Copperfield. 'I was born at Blunderstone, in Suffolk, or "thereby" as they say in Scotland . . . There is nothing half so green that I know anywhere, as the grass of that churchyard; nothing half so shady as its trees; nothing half so quiet as its tombstones.'

It is thought that by 'The Rookery, Blunderstone' Dickens meant Blundeston House which Sir John Soane designed for Nathaniel Rix and which was finished in 1786.

The seaside resort M. R. James had in mind for the town he invented in 'Oh, Whistle and I'll Come to You, my Lad' was Felixstowe. He called it Burnstow. 'Bleak and solemn was the view on which he took a last look before starting homeward . . . the squat martello tower, the lights of Aldsey village, the pale ribbon of sands intersected at intervals by black wooden groynings, the dim and murmuring sea.'

In fact, the martello tower at Slaughden is the biggest as well as the northernmost of these towers along the English coast. Burnstow appears again in 'The Tractate Middoth' and the sinister Squire Eldred lives at Bretfield which by changing a single letter we can identify as Bredfield where George Crabbe the younger lived and had his expensive vicarage.

Blundeston Church

AN ANTIQUARY AND ANCIENT PLACES

'Everyone who has travelled over eastern England knows the smaller country houses with which it is studded – the rather dank little buildings, usually in the Italian style, surrounded with parks of some eighty to a hundred acres. For me they have always had a very strong attraction: with the grey paling of split oak, the noble trees, the meres with their reed beds, and the line of distant woods.'

This is Montague Rhodes James beginning 'The Ash Tree', one of his 'Ghost Stories of an Antiquary'. He must have had Suffolk houses in mind and perhaps it is not too presumptuous to guess that when he wrote those lines he was thinking of Livermere Park.

Certainly he was one of those who travelled over eastern England. James wrote an outline of principal antiquarian features in the two counties in his book 'Suffolk and Norfolk', and he claimed to have visited 1,279 parishes. But Livermere Park was the house he knew best, for when he was a child he must have seen it every day.

He was brought up in the village, where his father was Rector, in a house now called Livermere Hall and had his home there from 1865 to 1909. In 1820 the old red brick front of Livermere Park had been encased in white Woolpit tiles – an act which James himself called 'disastrous' – and was demolished altogether a hundred years later. James also lamented the loss of the hall and of the great oaks in its park.

Inside the thatched church of St Peter are bench ends clumsily carved, certainly not the cunning and skilful craftsmanship which inspired those he describes in 'The Stalls of Barchester Cathedral'. For their models he must have looked elsewhere, but not too far away – perhaps to Dennington or Fressingfield?

'The prayer desk is terminated at the eastern extremity by three small but remarkable statuettes in the grotesque manner. One is an exquisitely modelled figure of a cat, whose crouching posture suggests with admirable spirit the suppleness, vigilance and craft of the redoubtable adversary of the genus Mus. Opposite to this is a figure seated upon a throne . . . but it is no earthly monarch whom the carver has sought to portray . . . The hand which rests upon his knee is armed with talons of horrifying length and sharpness. Between these two figures stands a shape muffled in a long mantle . . .'

There is a deserted village at Livermere, a name which has nothing to do with livers but probably derives from laefer or irises which grow along with bulrushes in the great lake, the mere. It is on the borders of the Breckland and there is an abandoned church too which retains Anglo-Saxon features. Aerial photographs show the outline of a former very long village street. None of this can be seen from the ground, only a

Great Livermere

farm with a garden full of roses and beyond it the desolate church, overhung with ivy which has trunks and branches like forest trees.

This is the edge of the Breckland, that curious stretch of country of empty stony fields and ancient deciduous woods, deserted villages and fallen churches. The Breckland has been re-afforested with conifers and much is lost of that forlorn atmosphere and agoraphobic sensation of panic Julian Tennyson experienced in the 1930s when he felt he was '. . . loose in some vast flat limitless arena, that all about you, beyond your sight, there is something which you most desperately want, and that if you run all your life and in any direction, you will never reach it.'

It is still possible to drive through the deep woods of the south Breckland and come to Hengrave Hall. Most of the great houses of Suffolk were built of brick or even of lath and plaster on a timber frame. Hengrave is partly of white brick from the brickfields of Bury Abbey but also of stone in a county where no natural stone was available. This freestone came from quarries in Northamptonshire and some from dissolved abbeys at Ixworth, Burwell and Thetford. The wealthy cloth merchant who built it had ambitions for a palace. It is said that he wanted to see its rich ornamentations multiplied by reflection in water, but the moat is gone now.

He was Sir Thomas Kytson. His family of Old Catholics once possessed Hengrave and maintained their own priest. The house is early Tudor. Building began in 1525 and is thought to have been inspired by Hampton Court. Elizabeth I came here and of course slept here in the Queen's Chamber at the top of the great stairs. The family chapel is now a church. It has become an ecumenical centre, busy with nuns and Christian laity, but standing outside the house in its spacious courtyard, the visitor is irresistibly reminded of 'Brideshead

Revisited' and half expects to hear that music float out from a mullioned window with its sweet, piercing, Purcell-like cadences.

John Wilbye, the madrigalist, lived in this house for thirty years from about 1595, master of the music for the household. 'Adieu, sweet Amaryllis' and 'Draw on, Sweet Night' are among his songs. There is a Wilbye Chamber in the house which was his room. Sir Philip Sidney was a frequent visitor at Hengrave and poet and musician must sometimes have met under its handsome roof.

Great Livermere
(opposite)

James's Church

The gardens at Hengrave

Hengrave Hall (opposite)

PLOVERS IN THE BORDER COUNTRY

O ver the hill from Honey Tye going south-west, the views begin. Stoke church, which is such a glorious landmark, stands high to the north. When the sun is shining but low in the sky is the best time to see this view, and in early winter. The poplars which grow here in profusion cast long thin shadows over the meadows above the river.

A narrow lane is the main road from here to Bures. This is the county border and, taking the by-roads, the traveller dodges in and out of Essex over the little hump-backed Stour bridges. In spite of the old halls and holly trees, it is not at all typical Suffolk. Weatherboard has begun and there are timber houses as well as barns. The flat land rolls into shallow hills, then steep ones.

It is a high climb up here. The countryside might be moors in the middle of England. Slowly huge views spread out and seem to encircle the winding road, until the top is reached, High Fen, a crossroads where in the bleak Middle Ages a gallows must have been, though history does not tell us so. The tilting green wheatfields are streaked in long lines by the harrow. Here and there towering Wellingtonias and Douglas firs shelter an isolated farmhouse. The drop into Bures is a dip and a swoop between copses of oak which keep their brown leaves long into the winter.

Half in Essex, half in Suffolk, Bures has a narrow bridge

spanning the Stour. St Mary's church is big and stately, its clock a little too large for its square pinnacled tower, seeming so perhaps because it once carried a spire. St Edmund was crowned in a church here in 855, site unknown, but there is a wooden effigy of him in St Mary's.

The road back to Nayland is worth driving along both ways. The views are the best in south Suffolk and worth seeing from each direction. Churches with square towers or stubby Essex spires stand on the horizon. Wormingford lies beyond the Stour, on the other side of a small bridge with white railing, houses weatherboard and half-timbered. St Andrew's church is big and handsome for this small village. The river flows broad and deep with pollarded willows on its banks.

Wissington or Wiston, which name you prefer is what you call it by. The local people, those whose families have always been here, call it Wiston. It is always grouped with Nayland, Nayland-with-Wissington, but for a few years now the main road from Colchester to Sudbury has separated the two. Nayland is almost a town, Wissington a tiny hamlet in the bottom of the river valley. But while Nayland church was for a long time a chapel of ease within the parish of Stoke-by-Nayland, Wissington has been a parish since parishes were first recorded.

Everything is small but the enormous corn stores. They are

Bargeboard Cottage

a sign of the times and as is so often the case these days, when observing and admiring our countryside, we have to learn when to look and when to close at least one eye. The corn stores behind us, it is possible to look with delight at diminutive ancient Wissington.

The Hall was built by Soane in 1791 for Samuel Beechcroft, a director of the Bank of England. St Mary's Church is more or less in its garden and is tiny enough for that. It is a perfect Norman church, of tripartite design, which Pevsner says was 'unfortunately' made more Norman in 1853. Some terrible things were done at Wissington and some absurd things too. But the Victorians made a very nice door to replace the original in the south doorway, apparently an exact copy.

The two chancel arches are Norman and the windows on the north wall are original Norman work. A very nasty face in stone with snarling lips and savage teeth glares down from the second arch. Paintings said to be of the 13th century adorn all the walls in the nave, one of which is thought to be the earliest representation of St Francis in English art. Skilled uncovering might reveal more under the lime wash. To the visitor, unlearned in such things, the wall paintings look pale and dim, vague, misty depictions in milky fawn and thin terra cotta. Over the north door is a dragon, probably not one of those six-hundred-year-old originals but a century or two younger, painted there when dragon legends were very fashionable in the Stour Valley.

By contrast to these ancient and delicate murals, hideous stained glass in harsh colours assaults the eye from the windows on the south side. All that can be said in favour of these windows is that the Victorian child who studied them could have been in no doubt that the Holy Land was a hot country sweltering under a fierce sun in a cobalt blue sky. The sad thing is though Dowsing left Wissington windows alone, later

meddlers did not. The glass in them, if not fine, was rare. Their removal was brought about not at the time of the dissolution of the monasteries nor by Cromwell, but by a zealous 19th century clergyman, one of the new reformers whose peers, at the same date of 1832, were setting up the Oxford Movement up the road at Hadleigh.

Charles Edward Birch M.A. came to be incumbent of the parish of Wissington in that year and at once set about the restoration of his church. He destroyed the old glass. But perhaps his intervention in other areas preserved St Mary's and ensured its survival, for he persuaded his wealthy friends to pay for all sorts of improvements. It was Mr Birch who uncovered the wall paintings.

'Norman' benches, pulpit, communion rails and reading desk were added. A mock mediaeval gallery, though an anachronism, was at least made by local craftsmen. In the 1930s wax was put on the wall paintings in a mistaken attempt to preserve them. It kept the damp in with unfortunate results. If you buy a guide or a postcard you put your money in a chest which stands in the porch. It seems to be mediaeval, has three locks, one for the vicar and one each for the churchwardens.

The war memorial in the churchyard shows that no less than four men from this tiny parish were killed in the First World War. As you walk away down the drive towards the gates you can see on the horizon the handsome buildings of the Jane Walker Hospital, once a tuberculosis sanatorium. Jane Walker was one of those women doctors who had to go to France for their medical training before it was permitted here. She pioneered the fresh air treatment for diseases of the lungs.

The air feels very fresh on these undulating hills. Lapwings, a kind of plover, called the farmer's friends, are everywhere in the fields, or flying high in black and silver flocks.

The Norman church at Wissington

The painting on the wall

Ancient stones at
Wissington (opposite)

The church at
Wissington (opposite)

A door in the church at
Wissington

67

ALL THAT LIES ON THE BANKS OF THE STOUR

Two English painters came from Suffolk, within 14 miles of each other on the river Stour, Constable from East Bergholt and Gainsborough from Sudbury. If Turner had been a native of this valley instead of London we should have had the triumvirate.

Thomas Gainsborough was born in 1727, most probably in the house in Gainsborough Street which is now a gallery for his work. They are proud of their painter in Sudbury and have given his name to their cinema, one of their bookshops, a garage, an estate agent, a fabric shop, a chemist, a company of silk weavers and a studio. Cast in bronze by MacKennel, he stands on Market Hill outside St Peter's Church, wearing his wig and tailcoat and holding brush and palette, as if about to paint the Black Boy Inn.

A story is told of his having forged his father's name to a note asking the schoolmaster to 'give Tom a holiday'. John Gainsborough saw the forged note and said, 'The boy will come to be hanged!' but when shown the sketches his son had made during his hours of truancy, changed his view. 'The boy will be a genius!'

That has all the ring of myth and few facts are known of Gainsborough's early life. When he was 14 he was sent to London to study painting in the studio of John Hayman, came back to Suffolk four years later, moved to Ipswich and soon made the acquaintance of Philip Thicknesse, the Governor of Landguard Fort. On his commission Gainsborough painted his first important landscape, a view of the fort with figures and sheep in the foreground and the estuary of the Stour behind. They hung the painting up on a wall built of mortar mixed with sea water and it soon fell apart.

Gainsborough was married by this time. His wife was Margaret Burr who brought with her an annuity of two hundred pounds, no doubt very welcome. They seem to have been ill-suited. She fancied herself the daughter of exiled royalty and justified ostentation in her dress by declaring, 'I have some right to this, for you know I am a prince's daughter.' More probably she was the natural child of the Duke of Bedford. Her husband painted her and portraits of Margaret can be seen in Gainsborough's House in Sudbury.

This is one of the most charming of small art museums. Its attractions lie in the house itself as much as the paintings it contains. The great Gainsboroughs are all elsewhere but there are some interesting portraits and a fine large landscape with figures. The painter once said that 'there was not a picturesque

Stour Valley

clump of trees, nor even a single tree of any beauty, no, nor hedgerow, stem or post' in the neighbourhood of Sudbury not loved by him from his childhood. But for all that there was little sale for his landscapes and he turned, far more profitably, to portraiture.

The heart of the town is changed since Gainsborough's day but not spoiled. The early 19th century Town Hall is a handsome classical building, scene these days of a mystifyingly frequent series of antiques fairs. On its west side is a restored gateway to the old town gaol and the passage that passes in here to Sudbury's warren-like hinterland, is called Gaol Lane. The

Public Library is housed in the Corn Exchange building which dates from 1841 when it was built at a cost of £1,620. Above the pillars is sprawled statuary of labouring men, stronger, handsomer and certainly happier than the originals on which these idealised figures were based.

An ivory chess piece made in the Middle Ages was discovered during the conversion of the building in which the Britannia Building Society is now housed. Many of the shops still keep their splendid 17th century interior timbers, some with carvings like gargoyles or misericords. In St Peter's Church is a strange detail, a carving of an angel with a beard,

The Black Boy Inn,
Sudbury (opposite)

Thomas Gainsborough
by McKennel

and in St Gregory's on the green, a roof boss of a terrier dog which belonged to Simon Tebaud of Sudbury, Archbishop of Canterbury and Lord Chancellor. Simon had a clergyhouse here in the 14th century and its gateway is still standing, though much restored. In the Peasants' Revolt they chopped off his head and it is buried in St Gregory's vestry. These peasants cannot have been much like the glamorised figures on the library entablature – Daniel Defoe described Sudbury as 'very populous and very poor.'

Sudbury is rich in beautiful old houses, Tudor and earlier, wool halls and Georgian shop fronts, inns and ancient flint walls, stands of town dwellings in local white brick and silk weavers' houses. They still weave silk in Sudbury. Material for the Princess Royal's wedding dress was made here. In the 14th century the town was famous for the production of baize, bunting – and shrouds.

Perhaps the prettiest group of houses is in Friar Street, a clutch in pastels behind a cobbled court. In one of the cottages here persecuted Quakers used to congregate until they were permitted to build their Meeting House; another was a chillingly named house of correction.

The compilers of Sudbury's guide claim it as one of the most attractive of English towns. They do well not to mention its immediate environs which have been made hideous beyond belief by encircling industrial sites, ugly estates and a by-pass. In spite of the by-pass Sudbury on market days is as thronged and congested as any city centre. The streaming traffic must, by a subtle but relentless process, erode the fine old buildings which give the town its unique character. Down by the river, however, Gainsborough's picturesque clumps of trees and hedgerows still just about hold their own.

Flatford Mill has claimed Constable and his memory is more honoured there than in his birthplace. In any case, the house where he was born is long gone, though the studio he began using in 1802 still stands, part of the petrol station next to the post office. He went to school in Lavenham and then to Dedham Grammar School.

'I should paint my own places best,' he wrote. 'Painting is but another word for feeling. I associate my "careless boyhood" to all that lies on the banks of the Stour . . .' He liked the flat or gently undulating landscape, and the joy he took in the light of Suffolk is well known. He said he loved every stile and stump and every lane in his native village. Once he spent three weeks in the Peak District and later on visited the Lakes, but the grandeur of this mountain scenery left him unmoved.

Even among lovers of Constable, his religious paintings are ignored or unknown. He painted three. One is at Feering in Essex and another in Brantham Church near Manningtree. His Suffolk picture is an altarpiece 'Christ Blessing the Bread and Wine' which is still in Nayland Church. This painting was commissioned by Constable's aunt who promised to pay him in her will. She kept her word and left him £400. When it was stolen a few years ago – and, happily, recovered – the Nayland altarpiece was valued at £100,000. His uncle, David Pike Watts, an orthodox clergyman who seems to have disliked Constable's religious work, roundly castigated this one. He said it was a portrait of the painter's elder brother.

Dedham Vale today, almost two hundred years since Constable began painting its woods and pastures and Dedham's tall straight church tower, ('I have a kingdom of my own both fertile and populous,' he wrote, 'my landscape and my children') resembles its ancient prospect more nearly than at any time during the past century. The acres of matchstick poplars, grown as a crop and unknown in Constable's day, were felled by the gale and their shallow roots torn out of the ground. An ill wind . . .

A window in the Constable Country

THE MOLECATCHER'S DAUGHTER

—>•<—

'The reader will forgive a little expansiveness here,' writes M. R. James of Great Livermere, adding, 'from 1865 to 1909 the rectory was my home, if not my dwelling-place.'

I ask for similar indulgence. Polstead was half my home and sometimes my dwelling place from 1970 until 1983, and another house there has been both ever since.

Church and Hall stand side by side, not long ago concealed from the road at least in summer by the fine trees, mostly limes and chestnuts, almost a wood of them outside the church gates. Most of those trees went down in the hurricane, broken, crushed, twisted, wrenched apart. It was hard to believe next day, looking at this devastation, this entanglement of split tree trunks and torn branches knotted and bound in fallen electricity cables, that a wind had done it all.

The Electricity Board have promised to put the cables underground. New trees have been planted. You can see the church now from Water Lane. Sometimes, when the branches are bare, you can see the Hall, a large, simple and gracious Georgian house of pale-coloured bricks, timber-framed 16th century at the back.

The church of St Mary is small and lovely. It would be a

nice place to be married in. It is Norman, yet very light inside, with a white gleam about it. It may have the earliest surviving English bricks and, alone among Suffolk's mediaeval church towers, has a stone spire. William Dowsing, the Reformation iconoclast, broke up the old glass, forty-five pictures, no less.

Pond House, on the other side of the pond – Polstead means 'a place of pools' – was built in 1760. Its dovecote is said to hold the curious record of being the largest in the county. Corder's House, once called Street Farm, then Corders, now Street Farm again, is older, timber-framed, a big house at the foot of the hill which leads up to Polstead Green. I used to live in the thatched cottage near the top on the left hand side. When they thatched the roof in the late sixties they found among the old rotting straw a wasp nest as tall as a man.

In Street Farm once lived William Corder. He was hanged for murder in 1829 and the horrid detail of that event is that they bound an account of his crime in his own skin. 'He suffered at Bury,' James says laconically of him. In fact, he was the last man to be hanged there in public.

Later opinions have varied as to the chances of his guilt. Certainly he had been the lover, among many others, of Maria Marten. He had promised to marry her and run off with

Polstead Church spire

her from her father the molecatcher's house. Maria disappeared. The interest of her story and the undoubted reason for its survival as 'case' and melodrama, lies in her stepmother's dream. The second Mrs Marten dreamed that she saw Maria's grave in the Red Barn. This was a barn, now gone, not in itself red but turned to that colour by the rays of the setting sun. They dug in the Red Barn and found poor Maria's body. By this time William Corder was living in London, running a school and married to a respectable woman, who no doubt knew nothing about any of it. They arrested him and he spent his last night of liberty in an upper room at Cock Farm. This house which faces Polstead Green has been said by some to be haunted by Corder whose footsteps can be heard overhead.

In the week Corder was executed, two of his brothers, while drunk, drove their horse and cart into Polstead Pond and were drowned. What must that have been like for old Mrs Corder? It hardly bears thinking of, even at this distance of time.

There is a plaque by the side of the church that says Maria is buried close at hand. The two brothers in their horse and cart haunt the environs of the pond. The Rector of that time, no one knows why, drives down Rectory Hill in a carriage drawn by a headless horse. A band of ghostly friars inexplicably walks through the air where there was once a path before the road was cut. Well, maybe.

We have a newish pink-washed village hall, a marvellous new village shop entirely run on voluntary labour and a pub

The Coblers (opposite)

Corders House

77

called The Cock. Or more usually, Polstead Cock. In these parts they use the village name followed by the name of the inn, Boxford Fleece, Groton Fox, Stoke Black Horse.

Four hamlets comprise the parish: Polstead, Polstead Heath, White Street Green and Bower House Tye. White Street Green is where I live, half way to Boxford and on the side of the valley through which the flows the Box, a tributary of the Stour, a narrow, brown, sometimes rapid stream, fringed with alders. There used to be orchids but they have been lost to intensive arable farming.

My house is very old, certainly in part 400 years old. Its name Nussteads is from the Danish 'Knuds Sted' – Canute's Place. There was a Danish settlement close to the Box in 850 AD. Our Canute may have no connection with Canute the Great, he who is erroneously said to have bidden the waves recede, but he wasn't far from here. The last battle between the Saxons and the Danes, in which the latter were victors, was fought at Assington, five miles away. Canute the Great built St Edmund's church on the site.

We know the minimum age of our house because the parish register of St Mary's Polstead has the following entry, translated from the Latin of the then Rector, concerning his own marriage in the year 1549:

'John Greenwood Master of Arts and sometimes Fellow and Bursar of the College of St John, Cambridge, now Pastor of the Parish Church of Polsted, took to wife Joanna Lungley, daughter of Thomas Lungley, of Nusted and of the same parish, the 11th day of July, 1549.'

I have sometimes wondered what became of them two years later when the Protestant Edward VI died and Mary Tudor came to the throne. The Roman Catholic Church was restored and priests were required to put away their wives. Perhaps Mrs Greenwood adopted the recognised and after all only temporary expedient of pretending to be her husband's housekeeper.

The house is a Suffolk long house which means that, downstairs at any rate, you have to walk through all the other rooms to get to the room at the far end. The timbers are oak, split with age in just the same way as the timbers in Little Hall at Lavenham are split, and that house which is the headquarters of the Suffolk Preservation Society dates from 1419. So maybe ours is older than we think. There is no fine carving, though woodworm – but not deathwatch beetle – have drilled away and in places given a spongy cork-like appearance to the surface of studwork. A great smoke bay, shaped like a long funnel of brick, passes up through the centre of the house. Until we had the chimneys shut off with register plates, the cats used to climb up inside like Beatrice Potter characters and try to catch starlings on the roof.

Wild life abounds where we live. Most days we see a hare in the garden, often foxes. A pair of deer sometimes visits the wood. At present, among the bird life, we have resident, or as constant visitors: a kingfisher, a heron, a pair of green woodpeckers and a pair of lesser spotted woodpeckers, nuthatches and tree creepers, goldfinches and greenfinches. A flock of ten or twelve long-tailed tits flies through the garden from tree to tree. Owls are common, calling to each other at dawn. I saw one fly across the meadow with a captured mouse in its claws, pursued and attacked by swallows who seemed to resent its making a rare daylight appearance.

The butterflies are beginning to come back and last summer there were commas, a clouded yellow and a small copper, as well as the common tortoiseshells and peacocks that congregate on the buddleia, the 'butterfly bush'. Less pleasant are the hornets, peculiarly indigenous to Polstead. But the blue cat deals with them and, mysteriously, comes to no harm.

Thatch

GHOSTS AND ANGLO-SAXON PENNIES

—►●◄—

It has been described, through some confusion with the house at Borley in Essex, long ago destroyed by fire, as 'the most haunted rectory on the books of the Church of England'. Like the Holy Roman Empire, in its latter days neither holy, Roman nor an Empire, the Haywards' house at Polstead is no longer on the books of the Church of England, is no longer a rectory and there is some doubt as to whether a ghost has even been seen there.

Heard? Smelt? Felt even? The answers to those questions must remain vague and sensibly qualified. John and Marilyn Hayward who bought the house, now called the Old Rectory, in 1979, are sceptical about the hauntings and quite happy to live with the ghosts anyway. They find the history of their house more interesting than spirit visitants. Though modest, they are justly proud of the restoration they have done.

'I went round ripping things apart,' John says. 'Victorian additions mostly. We did the best we could to get it back to 1620. Oddly, it seemed as if the house told us what to do.'

Parts dating from the 15th century, it was modernised towards the end of James I's reign. When we think of the date as being about seven years after Shakespeare's death, it seems a long time ago. In the 18th and early 19th centuries Tudor meant rusticity, was out of tune with the Age of Reason and with classicism. Gables and half-timbering were covered up or, where possible, removed by Georgianisation. The Swan at Lavenham was virtually turned into a Victorian pub by a similar process. We find this in White, writing of another place in the county in the middle of the 19th century: 'Though the town has been much improved during the last 40 years, it still retains many of its old thatched houses with whitewashed fronts.' A new facade was contrived for Polstead Rectory. It was one of five houses in Suffolk to be faced with 'mathematical tiles', the kind of tiles that are imitation 'white' bricks, pallid and anaemic, which could be nailed to a timber frame.

The mathematical tiles are still there. The Victorian fireplaces have gone. In many rooms the studwork has been exposed and the garage, wonderfully timbered, has become the drawing room. The prettiest room in the house is above this, the old solar, now the Haywards' bedroom, light and airy and with fine green views.

John is an amateur but knowledgeable archaeologist. He has assembled a collection of artefacts unearthed in his grounds: Anglo-Saxon pennies from the time of Ethelred and Canute, a Roman buckle in bronze, bronze crotal bells worn by cattle which still ring with a clear musical note. John found a Papal Bull of a Pope who died in 1242: Gregory IX. He found an unusual Victorian marble on top of a molehill, Henry II halfpennies and farthings, shaped like half and quarter circles,

Discoveries at the Old Rectory

80

musket balls, rings and thimbles and a pilgrim's badge with the head of John the Baptist.

As to the ghosts -

'We had heard the stories so we expected things to happen and, frankly, they haven't happened. I waited in the cellar at midnight for things to happen but nothing did. My study is supposed to be the haunted room and there was something odd there. The floor is a bit uneven and if you walk across it the vibration sets things jingling and ringing. There was a sort of explosion in there one day.'

'I was working at the desk,' Marilyn says, 'and I heard a soft bang behind me and then the things began to jingle the way they do when anyone walks across the floor. Of course there was no one there. I got up and walked towards the corner and it was difficult because there seemed to be an area of resistance.'

One of the stories is of carriage wheels making a crunching sound on the gravel drive when no carriage is there. The Haywards have heard sounds like that. They have heard the sound of a vehicle arriving, the grind and scrabble of wheels on the stones, have looked out on an empty drive. They have smelt the notorious smell.

'When it happens it's in the hall,' John says, 'at the head of the cellar stairs. Not a terrible smell, you know, but not nice either. A fishy-gluey smell.'

Marilyn says, 'When someone mentions it or draws attention to it, it seems to fade. It's as if it wants to be identified and talked about. And once it's been noticed and people have remarked on it it's satisfied and it goes away. Once when John was ill in London my brother came over to look after the house. After I got home and he was at home in Ipswich he phoned me to say he could smell the fish-glue smell in his own house.'

No ghosts? No visible ghosts at any rate – except on one occasion. The Rectory roof was being replaced and the workmen who came from Chelmsford knew nothing of reputed hauntings. One of the men apologised to John for disturbing his guest in the little attic room. He had been up his ladder and seen someone with long white hair retreat from the window in apparent offence. John told him he had no guest staying in the house, there was nobody there.

'He said he felt a bit ill when I told him that and he refused to go back up there.'

Something once touched Marilyn. Whatever it was gave her a gentle pat. John had another strange experience.

'It was a summer morning and I was having a look at the alarm system. A couple of security engineers and two electricians were with me. My daughter had shut herself up in the kitchen and Marilyn was upstairs in the bathroom. We heard a voice calling. It called out, "John, John," I thought it was Marilyn calling me and I ran upstairs. She had heard it too. My daughter heard it and so did the four men. It seemed to fill the house, that call, it was all around us. Another time my son heard it calling John. Of course it need not have been me it wanted. John is a common name.'

Marilyn is sometimes alone in the house at night and minds this not at all, not even in a power cut. 'I minded more when we lived in a terraced house in London. We feel that our house has a protective atmosphere. There was an odd night when I woke up about three convinced I'd left the garden hose running. I went back to sleep and woke again, this time sure I'd left the ignition key in the car. I went down and got outside just in time to see someone drive a car in through our gates and back out again the moment he saw me. That's what I mean about protecting us.'

Oak tree at Polstead

FULL AND FAIR ONES, COME AND BUY

———►●◄———

And since to look at things in bloom
Fifty springs are little room,
About the woodlands I will go
To see the cherry hung with snow.

In the spring, about the last week of April, Polstead is white with cherry blossom. Housman was right and it does look like snow, thick and fluffy, dense and scented in the orchards, a veil of sprinkled snow in the woodlands where the trees are big and old, the flowers sparse and the fruit small. But there is no fruit blossom more lovely than the wild cherry. You can keep your much-vaunted apple and peach blossom. Cherry grows in a delicate pendulous spray of many single flowers, their petals fragile as frost, the leafshoots a crisp bronze.

Ours is cherry-growing country. Not Suffolk but specifically Polstead. Once there used to be a cherry festival held here on the Sunday nearest to the 19th of July. There are cherry orchards at Boxted and wild trees at Arger Fen but Polstead is where the best cherries grow and in quantity. No one seems to know quite why, not even the cherry farmers.

The Cock

Cherries first grew in Britain in about 100 AD. No doubt the Romans brought them as they are said to have brought plane trees and pigeons and a host of other things. One sometimes wonders if there was anything here before the Roman invasion. Cherries need a deep, freely drained soil, a subsoil free from gravel, and dislike east winds and the wet. Polstead is dry enough but we have our share of gales and there is so much gravel in the subsoil that the Layham pit is seeking to enlarge its gravel workings.

Denny Richardson, who grows more cherries than anyone else, says that success with them may be due to the way Polstead is sheltered, escaping the worst frosts and other excesses of weather.

'People in Hadleigh or Sudbury will come and tell me that hail we had must have done for my crop and I say to them, what hail was that then?'

He remembers the huge harvests of the past when as many as ten lorries would be lined up to collect cherries for sale in Ipswich and Bury and Sudbury. That was at the beginning of the Second World War when his father could get ninepence a pound – 'a top price'.

In 1933 two shillings and ninepence, the equivalent insofar as this can be measured of about 14p, would be paid for a stone of fruit – a penny a pound. His grandfather would drive his horse and cart to Colchester, pack the fruit into wicker baskets, twenty pounds in each, and put them on the train for London.

'When we were children and the fruit was in season we used to have cherry pudding. I can remember my mother making it. I can remember the taste of it. It was suet crust packed full of black cherries and boiled in a cloth. It was wonderful. When you cut it in slices it was a rich purple colour and it was good hot or cold.'

Polstead has given its name to a variety, the Polstead Black which bore a small sweet very dark fruit.

'My brother has one still growing in his garden,' Denny Richardson says. 'You wouldn't grow them commercially today – too small. It's getting a perilous business anyway. Cherries aren't easy, even in Polstead.'

He lost a huge crop two years ago when heavy rain came at the wrong time. When the fruit begins to ripen in June he gets up to watch over it at four in the morning.

'Those days are gone when you could employ a bird scarer for a shilling a day.'

In decimal terms that, of course, would be 5p. The bird scarer would start at four and still be there until it got dark eighteen hours later, seven days a week. I have seen people with only one or two trees cover them entirely with nets when the fruit is ripening. This is hardly practicable for those with orchards. Scarecrows are sometimes put in trees to deter the birds. I doubt if as a method it works.

North American forests are celebrated for the brilliance of their colours in the autumn. The scarlet comes from the maples and the sumac. Our autumn colours are yellow and brown and our variety of maple has foliage that changes to gold rather than red. The only tree we have whose leaves turn red is the cherry. They darken to a rich crimson and colour the woods, as red as their fruits are in summer.

GREEN VISITORS

——▷●◁——

Round about the time they were building Gilbert de Chastelyn's castle at Lindsey, in the middle of the twelfth century, something very strange was happening in another part of the county. The green children were making their appearance.

'Nor does it seem right,' wrote William of Newburgh, 'to miss out a miracle unheard of for centuries which is known to have happened in Anglia in the reign of Stephen . . . four or five miles it is said from the noble monastery of the blessed King and Martyr Edmund.'

This was Woolpit. In high summer workers in the harvest fields came upon two children, a girl and a boy, who came out of one of the pits which are a feature of the landscape. The children were not only dressed in green but had green faces and bodies. They were taken to the house of a local landowner Sir Richard de Culne but would neither speak nor eat. All bread was refused. At last they found something they were willing to eat, the pith from the inside of beanstalks.

When they consented to speak they said they came from the land of St Martin, where there was perpetual twilight, had wandered into a cavern and drawn on by the sound of music, they found themselves in Woolpit, the land of bright light across the broad river. The cavern closed behind them.

The children were baptized but soon afterwards the boy died. The girl who 'was not much different from our own women' is later said to have married a man from King's Lynn.

Legend? Fairy story? William of Newburgh and Ralph of Coggeshall both vouched for its truth. So who were these children and why were they green? Perhaps they were waifs cast out of their own community on account of their strange appearance which may have been attributed to some sort of demonic possession.

My doctor friend, suddenly fascinated by this affair, tells me they may have been suffering from one of three forms of jaundice. Any type would be potentially fatal. We are not told how old they were, but since William of Newburgh passes on quite quickly to the girl's marriage, may we conclude that when found they had reached puberty? If this were so it might have played a part in the girl's recovery from haemolytic jaundice, while the boy would have had no such physiological therapy but perhaps succumbed to gallstones. Or, if the food given the children in Sir Richard's household was really unfamiliar, the effect of it on the boy might have been to precipitate a haemolytic crisis and quickly kill him.

What was the attraction of bean pith? The OED defines the condition called Pica as 'a perverted craving for substances unfit for food'. Or there is a possibility that the green children suffered from vitamin deficiency and craved vitamin C.

As to St Martin's land, the twilight and the cavern, the answers to these mysteries will never be known. The children may simply have been having their hosts or captors on.

Woolpit, where it all happened, is a village best known for

Ancient visitor

The church porch
(opposite)

the white bricks which used to be made there. Its name has nothing to do with wool but perhaps some connection with wolves, and the pits may be of Roman origin, excavated for the purpose even then of finding brick earth. The white bricks were once immensely fashionable and popular, 'equal in beauty to stone,' wrote White in 1844. The Tsar of Russia requested that a sample of them be sent for his inspection. Curiously, most of Woolpit's own houses are half-timbered or of old red brick.

St Mary's church is large and flint-walled, 15th century, but with a 19th century spire very unusual in Suffolk and more like the sort found in the Nene Valley. A much earlier spire blew down in one of those previous hurricanes, the great storm of 1703, to be replaced five years later. St Mary's double hammer beam angel roof is very famous and has been called the finest in the county. The roof stands on wall posts which in their turn rest on brackets of angels with wings spread out like alighting birds, so many that it would be a daunting task to count them.

The brass eagle lectern is in such good condition as to look new but in fact it was a gift of Elizabeth I. Strange carved animals squat on the bench ends, some 19th century but most very old. They are heraldic beasts and other fabulous creatures, winged or with serpentine tails, wyverns, basilisks, cockatrices perhaps. But they all have an amiable look, their faces those of friendly dogs, and the visitor is tempted to stroke a glossy head. The Lady's Well, not far from the church, used to be visited by pilgrims. Its water cured bad eyes.

The beast with a leaf in its mouth

The silver way (opposite)

CASTLINGS HALL

Kersey and Lindsey are where the wool came from. If nowhere else, characters in historical novels of the romantic kind still wear clothes made of linsey-woolsey and kerseymere. Shakespeare knew of these villages. Forswearing 'taffeta phrases and silken terms precise', Berowne in 'Love's Labour's Lost' vows in future to express his wooing in 'russet yeas and honest Kersey noes'. The Kersey Brook is forded in the village street but, higher up, descending from Milden where it rises, it flows through the bailey of Lindsey Castle, a moated mound now overgrown with oaks and hawthorn and brambles.

Lindsey was one of three castles, the others being at Offton and Milden, built to defend the little townships during the Interregnum of 1135 to 1154 when the throne of England was in dispute between Stephen and Matilda. At that time the population of the county of Suffolk was probably not much more than 70,000. The building of these great defensive earthworks would have involved an enormous work force, perhaps as many as a thousand men labouring for two years.

What remains of them cannot be accurately dated, nor their original form guessed at. But the observer has no need to be an archaeologist to see that this tree-crowned hummock is no natural feature of the landscape. The local people call it Boar Hill. Up through the soil, to be picked up and contemplated with awe, still come fragments of shells from oysters which must have been one of the staples of the defenders here,

and among the flints lie innumerable shards of roof tile which the earth endlessly disgorges.

The castle covers six acres and inside the dry moat there may once have been an Iron Age settlement. In a meadow nearby are two long ridges called manorial banks covering another six acres, and all this land the farmer is forbidden to cultivate by a Department for the Environment preservation order. 20 acres of the 400 which constitute the farm of Castlings Hall may not come under the plough and these meadows are grazed by a herd of Blonde d'Aquitaine cattle, corn-coloured or fairer, draft oxen from south-western France.

The lordship of this manor – Castelyns in Groton in the County of Suffolk – seems first to have been held by a knight called Sir Gilbert de Chastelyn who died in 1294. Through his descendants it passed to the Knyvet family and from them to the Cloptons, once owners of Kentwell Hall and remembered for the Clopton Chantry in Long Melford Church. Fifty-five tombs of the Clopton family are recorded there, though more than half now are lacking their brass portraits. Among cameo epitaphs, was there ever a more fulsome one than this?

'Bountiful and liberal and skilled and proficient in all the arts, famed for his gentle blood, William Clopton is confined in this narrow tomb, but all too straight for so great a friend of virtue.'

Since it is in the late Elizabethan style, it would seem that the present manor house of Castlings was built during the

Castlings Hall

latter half of the 16th century. If there was an earlier house here when William Clopton, grandson of the Kentwell paragon, began the work in or around 1560, and there seems to have been from remnants in the present building, it was probably that mentioned in ancient documents as 'the tenement called Castelains.'

The farmer and present Lord of the Manor of Castlings is Sam Block who came there 20 years ago. As well as his sleek golden cattle he keeps peacocks which strut in the farmyard and flounce shrieking up on to the walls. At midsummer there were thirteen grown peafowl and three or four sets of young as well as a sprawled beady-eyed peahen lolling on her eggs in a manger. The roof of the house was being re-tiled, repairing the damage done by the hurricane when twelve oaks fell on Castlings land.

The hall is gracious and beautiful and deserved better than to be disguised as a Georgian farmhouse, the fate destined for it by modernisation in the late eighteenth or early nineteenth century. The jettied first floor seems to have been underbuilt, the mullions replaced with sash windows and the exterior plastered. In the process of this Georgianisation the timberwork must have been much cut about. But it is still possible to see the carved bressumers and brackets, the sills and the buttresses, redeemed from desecration. A very pleasing restoration was carried out in the early 1930s by the architect Basil Oliver, himself an East Anglian. The windows in particular were made to reassume their ancient structure and height.

'I specially liked its friendliness when I first came to the house,' Sam Block says. 'The ceilings are high, fairly unusual in houses of this sort of age, and the rooms are lit by so many windows.'

Light pouring into the rooms, an airiness unexpected in a Tudor manor, is what you notice first at Castlings. It is very nearly, like Bess of Hardwick's, a house of 'more window than wall'. Then the quiet of the place is felt, the stillness.

Those unfamiliar with very old houses always want to know if they are haunted. It is the first question they ask: 'Is there a ghost?' Only a very insensitive visitor, or one with a lust for sensation in unlikely circumstances, would suspect hauntings here. Even in the oldest part, where unexplained cavities between the studs lead investigators to believe in a Plantagenet predecessor, an atmosphere prevails of tranquillity. There are no ghosts here, but rather the sense of a placid past.

William Clopton, its builder, stayed only a short time. It was his grandson, an Essex man, who went off to Virginia in the early seventeenth century and became the progenitor of the 400 or so Cloptons in the United States today. Eighty of them came to tea at Castlings a few years back, all Clopton descendants.

They have produced a grand and very weighty book of pedigrees which traces their descent back through one dusty line after another to such forgotten notables as Ingelar Count of Anjou in 870 AD, Henry III of England and a figure who sounds mythical but may not be, St Arnulf Bishop of Metz. It is all great fun and perhaps most of us, given the time and inclination, could do the same.

Castlings is hard to find. It is only 70 miles from London, yet it lies in some of the deepest country England has. Lanes meander to it between fields hedgeless and steeply hedged, past mysterious little woodlands. You can see Kersey church from Castlings' meadows, its tower with the parapet ornamented in stone and flint, tall on its steep little hill. The parish is Groton where Winthrop came from, the first Governor of Massachusetts. Lindsey, up the road, has the ancient St James's Chapel, a national monument with a thatched roof, and a pub at each end of the village, The White Rose and The Red.

Bressumer at Castlings

SPIRELET

The Sciapod

The Dennington Pyx
(opposite)

96

The church at Dennington is full of treasures. It is like a museum in that it is hard to believe that all these things are there, not because someone made a collection of them but because they happen to belong there.

Among the mediaeval bench end carvings is the Sciapod, member of a mythical race of giants from Libya who had one webbed foot apiece. Pliny said the Sciapodes had 'great power and pertinence in leaping' but this one lies on his back, using his foot as an umbrella, and clutching two little headless creatures under his arm. The benches date from the 15th century and have carved backs and 76 intricately carved ends, all of which are different. Among the armrests are an angel, a mermaid, a pelican with her young, a lion, a tortoise, and a two-headed eagle.

A tomb commemorates Sir William Phelip, Lord Bardolph, not one of those gentlemen in England who held themselves accursed they were not there but a companion in arms of Henry V at Agincourt. He and his wife are in effigies of alabaster, he with his feet on an eagle and she with hers on a wyvern. Very ancient chancel windows have carvings on their capitals of dainty little leaves and owls' faces. There is a sand writing table which was used in the 19th century to teach children to write. The curious pulpit is a three-decker structure, two storeys with a kind of mezzanine floor, and the Peter's Pence box, cut out of a solid block of oak, still stands where it has been standing for 700 years. Two parclose screens are complete with lofts and staircases.

There is lots of old glass, decorative only and without pictures. Of the modern glass – not quite so modern today – M. R. James said severely that it was 'absolutely vile'.

He has no comment whatever to make on the pyx canopy. Before the Reformation the Blessed Sacrament was kept in a silver receptacle or pyx which was shrouded in a cloth and hung above the high altar. There are no longer any pyxes in any Suffolk churches, the Exning pyx having long ago disappeared. Hessett, to the east of Bury, has a precious fragile pyx cloth of drawn thread work with a silk fringe, now on permanent loan to the British Museum. Such a cloth wrapped the face of Mary Queen of Scots before she laid her head on the block.

The pyx canopy at Dennington may be the only one in the country, one of only two of its kind in Europe. Scholars have hotly disputed the legitimacy of the one at Wells, for instance. Certainly the wooden cylinder of Wells is not much like the carved spirelet which hangs shrouded in its coarse modern sindon in the sanctuary of St Mary's Dennington. It is 55 inches long, eight-sided, with crockets at the angles terminating in a finial. Its sides are painted red and green alternately and the finials are painted gold. It is impossible to say whether it is beautiful, except insofar as we seem to take it for granted that anything over 200 years old is beautiful. This pyx canopy is nearly three times as old as that.

So greatly were pyxes venerated that invading armies crossing Europe respected them. You can stand in the aisle at Dennington and look at this one, or at least at the vessel which holds a replacement, virtually unprotected as it is. It looks a bit like a chandelier done up in a linen bag to keep out the dust. Its function signified that God was inside. No wonder the soldier, bent on pillage, regarded it with an awe that was superstitious or reverent, according to one's viewpoint.

Bench ends at Dennington

A GENTLE HOUSE

————▶●◀————

It is a dove-grey house, quite large, of gracious proportions, which stands in a park of some 40 acres. The drive that leads to it from the Wattisham road describes a shallow elegant curve, so designed as to give the visitor a gentle surprise when its walls come into view behind the black spreading arms of a majestic cedar.

Bentons is gentle. If it were necessary to think of another adjective the word 'gracious' would follow close upon it. The Oxford Dictionary devotes almost a column to definitions of 'gentle' but among them are: 'of excellent breed or spirit', 'cultivated', 'not harsh or irritating to the touch, soft, tender, pliant, supple.' Something of an air of these qualities combined seems to lay upon the approaching visitor a hand that is – gentle.

The house will never find its way into any guidebook. It is not even listed. Scores, if not hundreds, very like it were built in the middle of the nineteenth century. But only England ever produced them, and no later architectural fad or phase has ever imitated them. Along with the gentleness of Bentons, its pearly colour and the soft, subdued sheen of its brickwork, goes its indisputable Englishness. Herbaceous borders form its English garden. A table and chairs under the cedar tree are waiting for tea to be served on the lawn. Its walls are austere in winter and mellow in summer and its windows glow with the deep dark gleam only seen in old glass.

It was built as the rectory of Bildeston in 1850. Joseph Gedge, the Rector, built the house on the site of an earlier one in what was known as the Italian style, though today we would probably call it Palladian for its bow windows and pillared portico, a style that was rapidly going out as the Gothic came in. A kind of brick called gault was used, being composed of a substance somewhere between clay and marl. The park was created out of the glebe land and the remainder of the estate farmed out, the rents contributing to the priest's income.

But in 1917 the incumbent of the parish threatened to resign the living because of the inconvenient and dilapidated condition of the house. Another parsonage was bought and the house sold on condition that the new owner should re-name it, any version of 'Old Rectory' being unacceptable to the Church of England. He called it Bentons, choosing this not because, as is often supposed, there was some connection with Benton Street in Hadleigh, but for the most prosaic of all reasons, that the house he had come from in Kent bore that name.

I saw Bentons first in the pen and ink drawing which is the motif on the note cards Maureen and Monty Baker-Munton send to their friends. At that time they were set on moving out of it and into a house they had bought at Hawkedon near Bury St Edmund's. When they had first come to Bentons, a friend who knew the house said to Maureen:

'My dear woman, there's Bentons! It'll kill you.'

But that had been 25 years before. Now they felt Bentons was too much for them, too cold in winter and its grounds too

The cedar – stricken but surviving

100

large. It had not killed them, they had thrived on it and it had flourished in their care; they had transformed it, but now . . .?

People seldom take advice, even when they ask for it. I drove up the shallow elegant drive and saw the dove-grey house, went inside and saw the staircase winding in wide curves up towards the lantern in the highest ceiling. I saw the drawing room and stepped out through the raised sash window to walk under the cedar – and I told them not to move. They would regret moving and then it would be too late. They took my advice and stayed and now they tell me they are grateful.

It is the most beautiful drawing room I know. That is, it is the most beautiful drawing room of reasonable, quite small, proportions in a private house in which people live active, full lives, give parties, and whose floors they tread and whose chairs and tables they touch without extravagant care. It is a room that seems always either full of sunshine or radiant with firelight.

The windows are the original curved eight-ounce glass of 1850 but for two panes blown out in the hurricane. That same night the Corsican Pine went down and a great limb blew off the cedar. Wounded but still a vast awesome tree, it is what you look out on when you stand in the floor-deep bow window between curtains of corn-coloured silk, the smooth parkland behind it and the gently folded pastures beyond.

'I don't know how many windows we've got,' Maureen says. 'I try counting the windows in this house like counting sheep but I always fall asleep before I finish.'

Wooden shutters are closed every night. They are the originals and provide a kind of alternative double glazing as well as security. When they have been folded over the windows Bentons feels snug. The Baker-Muntons spent six months getting the paint off these shutters and exposing the wood beneath. They restored the semi-derelict house them-

selves. As a housewarming present, friends came and papered their bedroom.

'They taught us how to decorate. All we could afford then was to have the ceilings done professionally. It didn't kill us because we loved it and it was fun, like a game. Later on an architect came here and admired it. He said it was right that we hadn't put in en suite bathrooms and that sort of thing.

'We had no big furniture and when we started buying we made a rule never to pay more than two pounds ten – well, two pounds fifty it would be now – for anything. Monty bought some great oils in gilt frames and we told people they were portraits of his ancestors. I think they were really the mayor and mayoress of Edinburgh. He found a square piano chucked out into one of the pens in the cattle market at Stowmarket and bought it for fifteen bob. It turned out to date from 1807. The restorer worked on it for fifteen months.'

The piano which now stands in the drawing room is a six-legged upright, pale gold in colour and inlaid with satinwood. It stands against a wall on which hang abstract landscapes by John Addyman, two John Barber landscapes, two Cavendish Morton watercolours and a miniature Christine Hart-Davies. There is a lovely gouache by Fritz Gross of his daughter in a picture hat.

Monty's favourite is the Ernst Laub painting 'En Lille Pige', which they call the Little Danish Girl. He bought a seven-piece Victorian suite in a junk shop and kept within their expenditure limit. Maureen made all the curtains, covered the chairs. The three lamps are Royal Doulton vases in a lacy design of turquoise, white and bronze.

In the hall hangs a flower piece in oils that looks enough like a Fantin-Latour to make it easy to understand why Maureen wanted it. She and Monty first saw it in a shop in Spain in the sixties. They were there on holiday at the time of the extreme currency restrictions when £25 was all holidaymakers were allowed to take out of the country. With £15 of this left between them, the asking price was far beyond their means.

The shopkeeper had been too distracted for much intense bargaining by the failure of an out-worker to make two lamp-shades which had been ordered. Monty, inspired, said,

'My wife will make them for you.'

And Maureen did. They travelled around the district on buses, collecting silk here, frames there, lace somewhere else. Maureen sat in their hotel room all weekend sewing the shades. She got her picture and they brought it home with them.

The gardens at Bentons are on the grand scale. Mowing the lawns is like what they used to say about painting the Forth Bridge, now probably say about the Golden Gate – as soon as you've finished you have to start all over again. The herbaceous borders need constant re-stocking. Maureen is very taken with lilies at present. She is planning to plant the large circular bed in front of the house with only blue and white flowers this year. The dove-grey porch is filled with red and yellow begonias summer and autumn-long.

The drawing room
at Bentons

THE ESTUARY OF
THE ALDE

——>●<——

George Crabbe is probably Suffolk's most distinguished literary figure. A respectable and hard-working country parson, he was born in Aldeburgh in 1754 and lived in Suffolk for the first third of his life. He was 'the poet of the poor' who wrote about the neighbourhood of the sea and the people of the coast, drawing character from life and unaware apparently that it was possible to create fiction from the imagination.

If his fame today rests principally on the opera Britten based on his poem 'The Borough', this is very much because he was a pioneer. Many followed where Crabbe led. Others came to understand what was new to writers of the 18th and early 19th centuries, that it was possible to write of common life without intending to amuse. Poor people were not by definition funny.

In his day Aldeburgh was a miserable and impoverished place. 'The Village', which has been called Crabbe's finest work, was written in part as protest against the sentimentality of Goldsmith's 'The Deserted Village'. He set himself in revolt against an eighteenth century convention of the innate nobility of the peasant and the enviable delights of the pastoral life. The seaboard of Suffolk was a 'frowning coast', its inhabitants the 'poor laborious natives of the place'.

'Where the thin harvest waves its withered ears;
Rank weeds that every art and care defy,

Reign o'er the land and rob the blighted rye:
There thistles stretch their prickly arms afar,
And to the ragged infant threaten war;
There poppies nodding, mock the hope of toil;
There the blue bugloss paints the sterile soil;
Hardy and high, above the slender sheaf,
The slimy mallow waves her silky leaf;
O'er the young shoot the charlock throws a shade,
And clasping tares cling round the sickly blade . . .'

Prosperity has arrived in latter-day Aldeburgh. Music has come and some of the finest craft work in the country, and tourism in its least aggressive aspect, vulgarity and noise happily absent. How Aldeburgh has succeeded in becoming a popular resort with hardly any of the drawbacks associated with seaside places, yet without Frinton's unnatural and artificial refinement, is a secret known only to the no longer poor but still no doubt laborious natives and perhaps to Suffolk County Council. Charming things go on there and almost every corner is delightful. E. M. Forster called it 'a bleak little place' but he liked it. Its name means 'old fort'.

They say Shakespeare may have performed in the church. Lord Leicester's actors played there in the summer of 1573. If Shakespeare did act at Aldeburgh it would have been 22 years after that, the year after A Midsummer Night's Dream was writ-

Fish shop on the beach

ten and while his company was playing at Ipswich. Wilkie Collins used the town as one of the settings for his novel 'No Name', calling it Aldborough.

'The sea showed it to her. Dimly distinguishable through the mist, she saw a little fleet of coasting vessels slowly drifting towards the house, all following the same direction with the favouring set of the tide. In half an hour – perhaps in less – the fleet would have passed her window. The hands of her watch pointed to four o'clock. She seated herself close at the side of the window, with her back toward the quarter from which the vessels were drifting down on her – with the poison placed on the window sill and the watch on her lap. For one half-hour to come she determined to wait there and count the vessels as they went by. If in that time an even number passed her, the sign given should be a sign to live. If the uneven number prevailed, the end should be Death.'

On the lawns above the shingle beach children come to watch Punch and Judy. There are too many antique shops but what pretty town in Suffolk is without them? Remove the discreet advertisements outside and the holidaymaker might take the cinema for some London weekender's home. It is a half-timbered 'black and white' house in the High Street, one of

Boats on the shingle (previous page)

Picture show at Aldeburgh

Sizewell – the first of several? (overleaf)

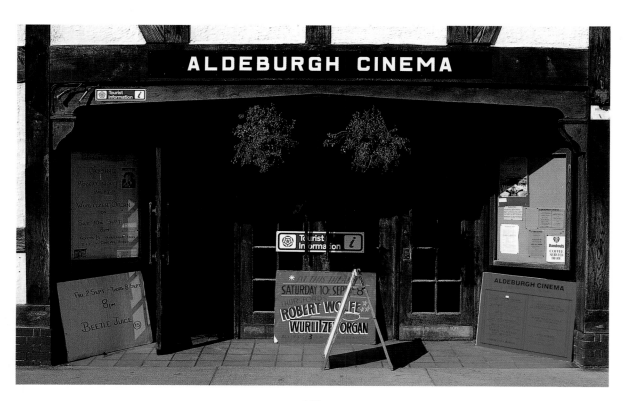

the oldest cinemas in the country, and it just manages to escape being quaint.

There are no cliffs, no headlands, only the silver sea and, to the north, Leiston among its trees. This was the birthplace, at Theberton Hall, of Charles Montagu Doughty, greatest of all Arabian travellers, who published in 1888 that curious book, written as if by an Elizabethan, 'Travels in Arabia Deserta'. At Orford the Alde becomes the Ore. They caught a merman there in the 13th century but not only could he not be converted to Christianity but refused altogether to speak. What was he really? They would have been used to seals. Perhaps a walrus. We may imagine an abbot preaching to him, monks solemnly swinging censers. It is good to know that he escaped his captors.

The rectangular shape in the far distance, divided by a vertical line like string round a parcel, the uninitiated might take for a block of flats put up while the planners' backs were turned. Pevsner describes it as 'clad in aluminium'. It takes on a sinister aspect, vague and insubstantial there in the luminous mist, only when you know that this is the nuclear power station at Sizewell. And a second is being built, a third planned.

Meanwhile, the sea which drowned Dunwich continues to erode this soft coast. South of the town, at Slaughden, it has taken the last remaining buildings. The early 16th century Moot Hall, now almost on the beach, was probably once in the middle of Aldeburgh, until the sea turned town centre into town rim. A long bank of shingle divides the Alde from the North Sea with a stepped concrete wall reinforcing the seaward side. The wall will not have to stand another winter's battering. The government has given the Anglian Water Authority approval for an urgent £4 million sea defence scheme at Aldeburgh and Orford.

Small solace though it may be, none of this is new. 'Two centuries and a half ago, Aldeburgh was a place of considerable importance,' says an authority of the mid-19th century, 'but repeated encroachments of the sea reduced it to the rank of a small fishing town. During the last century the ocean made great ravages, overthrowing many houses, together with the market-place and cross. A plan of the town in 1559 proves it to have been at that time of considerable magnitude, and represents the church as being at more than ten times its present distance from the shore . . .'

For all that, it was 'a delightful bathing place, pleasantly situated on the side of a picturesque acclivity, rising boldly from the German Ocean'. Since Crabbe's day the 'clay-built cottages, which gave to the place a mean and squalid appearance' have been replaced 'by neat and comfortable dwellings, and several large and handsome mansions, which are the occasional retreat of persons of rank and fortune'. There seems to have been sand on the beach at Aldeburgh then as well as pisum marinum, by the sound of it a kind of purple-flowered everlasting pea, on the fruits of which the poor survived during a famine in the 1550s. Sand and peas disappeared long ago.

The Aldeburgh Foundation has its headquarters here, its music shop and its club and restaurant, a hundred yards from the sea. On the other side of the courtyard, in the Peter Pears Gallery, the Suffolk Crafts Society holds its annual exhibition in July and August. It is hard to think of a pleasanter way of spending a fine summer's day than to climb the wooden staircase up to the exhibition, look at the beautiful things for half an hour, have a drink at a table outside the restaurant and go for a walk along the front. All that is needed to make it perfect is a magic wand to change the feet-punishing shingle, the sharpest and hardest in England, back into sand – and a new sea wall.

SHOP WINDOW

—▶●◀—

It is partly the intellectual snobbery of the fine arts world and partly the objects we all possess in the backs of cupboards, pokerwork photo frames and chocolate-glaze ashtrays, that have given crafts a bad name. Perhaps it would be better to find a new word for what craftsmen do and make, particularly what they do and make in Suffolk.

'This country is jammed full of crafts shops and crafts fairs,' says Heather Hyne, the Society's Treasurer. 'The difference is that our standard is tremendously high. We are designer craftsmen and we are putting superb designs and excellent quality before the public.'

Pottery, jewellery, wall hangings, lighting, work in wood and work in stone, book binding and silk painting, ceramic sculpture and batik. Of the exhibition she says, 'This is our shop window.'

It has an interesting effect on new visitors who simultaneously see that there is an alternative to commercially made objects and that these may be the less inviting option. Some things sell very fast and unless you get there in the first few days there will already be red stickers beside all Michelle Ohlson's ceramic clocks and candlesticks in their dark blue glaze, Holly Belsher's gold jewellery with baroque freshwater pearls and Rose Gilling's batik pictures. There is always a crowd in front of a Jill Essery embroidered and quilted silk sculpture or one of Donald Simpson's walnut tables.

The Society has 140 members and will be 20 years old in 1991. To be accepted you must be proposed and seconded by members, each of whom give their reasons for valuing your work. A selection of the results of your craftsmanship is submitted to the entire membership who vote on it and only a two-thirds majority admits you. About a third to a half of applicants get in.

'It's not like a gardeners' club,' says Heather Hyne, whose husband Reggie, an architect by profession and potter by inclination, is the exhibition designer. 'We're a group of professional people. This isn't a hobby.' And, sombrely, 'An awful lot of craftsmen live in poverty. We try to help people earn their livings.'

Of the 28 who applied last year, 10 were admitted. One of these was Jonathan Keep who must live and support his family by his craft alone. Teaching or any other employment is not open to him or his wife while they are in this country on annually renewable visas. They came here from South Africa in 1983 on a self-motivated educational tour, visited galleries and museums and decided they would like to be part of the crafts scene in this country. They were back again as immigrants a year later and came to Suffolk in 1986.

Charmaine Keep was admitted a member of the Society at this time as a weaver. She and Jonathan live in one of the cottages that are part of the Maltings complex at Snape Bridge. Their front room is their workshop where she has her loom and he his wheel and kiln. Their little dog is with them, sit-

The hands of
Jonathan Keep

ting in the deep embrasure of the window. It is a very small room in which to practise such divergent crafts, Jonathan working with clay next to a loom laden with tapestry.

'Between the flying clay and the fluff off rugs and the dog's hair,' says Charmaine, 'we have an interesting time.'

She dyes her own wool which hangs in hanks behind the loom, fuchsia pink and petunia purple, kingfisher and lime, scarlet and ultramarine, for the rugs and wall hangings she makes are distinguished by the brilliance of their colours. For her designs she goes to nature. 'Outside here at Snape I saw a partridge that had been killed on the road and its mate standing beside it under a tree, staring in such utter bewilderment. At the same time the pair of flycatchers we call our own were hatching out their five eggs. All that led to the design I made for the exhibition, Partridges under a Magic Tree.'

The Keeps love Suffolk but there is nothing of our green, grey-skied county in these designs which owe the glory of their colours to the tropics or perhaps to the Africa of her earlier days. She weaves without a pattern or a chart. 'I can't draw.'

The back of the work faces her as she weaves, and as she proceeds the finished fabric disappears, while the design as it will be is held in her head, mysterious but sure, to the watcher only the negative side of the tapestry revealed with its loose strands and its knots. Complete, it will be a gorgeous menagerie of fishes and birds, brighter than the spectrum.

Meanwhile, Jonathan is throwing his pots in his own version of the willow pattern: tea sets, a range of jugs, vases, plates, soufflé dishes. The domestic ware he makes is taken to the other side of the Maltings where it is sold in the crafts shop. Charmaine relies on direct sales and on exhibitions as a market for her own work.

The cold of Suffolk winters troubles them less than might be expected.

'The heat from the kiln keeps us warm. We work in here wearing tee-shirts in January, it gets so hot. People go by in the snow all wrapped up and stare in here at us in amazement.'

Charmaine and Jonathan Keep in their workshop (opposite)

Craftsmen's dog

SNAPE

The old hump-backed bridge at Snape, the port on the Alde, was the first victim of Sizewell. Narrow, single-arched, it had been built for horses and carts, not trucks. The present bridge, where the Maltings is – its address is Snape Bridge – was built, to the distress of conservationists, in 1960, some half dozen years before the conversion of the old buildings into what has been called one of the finest concert halls in Europe.

It is getting on for fifteen hundred years since the Saxon ship was buried at Snape. It had already been robbed when they dug it up out of Church Common in 1862 but interesting things were still to be found: vases and cloth and a gold ring and oddest of all, since there was no sign of a body, some auburn hair.

This is how White describes Snape in his Gazetteer of 1844: 'There is a good bridge and commodious wharf and warehouses, up to which the Alde is navigable for vessels of 100 tons burthen. About 17,000 quarters of barley are shipped here yearly for London and other markets by Mr Newson Garrett, who has warehouses etc on both sides of the bridge.'

Within ten years Newson Garrett had introduced malting, so that malt rather than its raw material might be shipped direct to the brewers. The final stage in the process was screening the malt in order to remove the roots from the grain. For this purpose Garrett built special malt houses, all to his own design. It is said that he drew the line of the buildings facing the road with a stick in the dust. The curve is still there today. Of these four malt houses, the most recent is that now converted into a concert hall.

The mellow red bricks were made at his own brickworks. Over the central archway he put his own initials and the date 1859. These buildings have been called unique among examples of 19th century industrial design.

Garrett liked to be on hand to supervise the malting, so he built a house there for himself, his wife and many children. They lived at Snape Bridge House at the southernmost end of the maltings for the winter and moved back to their home at Alde House in May when the malting seasons ended. His was a family of pioneers. He had ten children, six girls and four boys. Of the girls Elizabeth, the second daughter, became the first woman in this country to qualify as a doctor. Later on she became the country's first woman mayor, but some years previously had founded a hospital exclusively for women, the Elizabeth Garrett Anderson, in London's Euston Road.

One of her sisters was the suffragist Dame Millicent Garrett Fawcett; another became an interior designer, the first woman to set up in this line of business on her own. Two of the sons followed in their father's footsteps at Snape and at the Bow Brewery in London. Garrett went on building, a terrace in Aldeburgh, a private estate, big houses for his sons and daughters. He served three terms as Mayor of Aldeburgh. And, interestingly, he was passionately fond of music.

The Maltings

THE MALT HOUSE

—►●◄—

They say that the first field of sugar beet grown in Suffolk was sown and harvested a mile or so across the river. Dutchmen came over to tend the crop. Then what of the sugar beet factory set up in Lavenham nearly 40 years before in 1869? Whatever the truth of it is, they got down on their knees to thin out the plants in those days and dug the beet out by hand.

The Aldeburgh Festival, which is really the Snape Festival, was started in 1947 by Benjamin Britten, Peter Pears and Eric Crozier, with, later, Imogen Holst. Britten at that time had been living at Snape windmill, said to be the oldest dated windmill in Suffolk. There he wrote his masterpiece 'Peter Grimes'. It was his move to Aldeburgh (there is a plaque on the house in Crabbe Street where he lived) which engendered the Festival, created within what Norman Scarfe calls 'the admirable range of the Maltings'.

The conversion was made in 1966 and 1967 and the architect was Derek Sugden. The acoustics were said to be his special triumph. Two years afterwards, on the first night of the 1969 Festival, the concert hall burned down. On the morning of June 8 the roof lay in a heap of charred timbers and blackened iron on the ruined floor. But a year later it had been rebuilt. Since 1979 the Maltings Complex has also housed the Britten-Pears School for Advanced Musical Studies.

The red brick buildings are heavily hung with ivy. The timber work is creamy white. There is lots of new building, all blending, pastels and red, or with a bleached look like the marshes themselves. The estuary is what you see from the Maltings windows looking east, from the steps and the long terrace.

It is a very big sky. I have never seen it a clear blue but always combed with cream and silver or long streaks of red, and it is always moving. The grass is very green and then not green at all, but fair hair colour and salty grey. Silver-blue water lies in thin meres. There are hundreds of birds, redshank and shelduck, a heron sometimes, cormorants. On summer evenings, at a rare still hour, I have seen a white owl hunting low over the meadows.

The Maltings Concert
Hall (previous page)

Sunrise at Snape

THE EXTENDED VALLEY

—>•<—

Hadleigh is where I go shopping when I am in a hurry and don't want to go too far. It is like most English small towns in that – with two or three exceptions invidious to name – its shops leave much to be desired. You can compensate with the pleasure you get from looking at the place. It is easily as beautiful as Lavenham and far less frequented by tourists.

The name may mean 'heath meadow' or 'chief town' or 'extended valley'. Guthrum the Dane made Hadleigh his headquarters and was buried here in 889 AD. In the great days of wool it was the 14th most properous town in England with fine houses and a magnificent church. Students of church history know Hadleigh as the place where the Oxford Movement, which sought to restore Roman Catholic thought and practice to the Anglican Church, began in 1833. Hugh James Rose was Dean. He and his friends Froude, Palmer and Perceval, met here to discuss the church situation, the occasion becoming known as the Hadleigh Conference.

But where exactly did they meet? Some authorities say in the Deanery – the incumbent here, for some ancient and obscure reason, is called the Dean, though strictly he is not one – others that it was in the gate tower. The new Deanery had been built by 1831 in imitation Tudor, intended no doubt to match its surroundings. Probably the meeting was up in the Deanery Tower, in a room above the entrance. It was a situation which would have appealed to those passionate and feverish Anglo-Catholics.

Hadleigh people know it as Pykenham's Tower. They are justly proud of it and have its picture on their town sign at either end of the by-pass. It is a gatehouse, enormously tall, a red brick building with polygonal turrets and a four-centred archway. The centre and turrets are battlemented. It is in such good condition, so perfectly preserved just standing there beyond the church, that I am afraid, to my eyes, it looks as if some devotee of the Gothic and follower of Ruskin put it up in the 19th century. This may in part be due to the nasty chimneys which were stuck on in 1830. In fact it was built in 1495. It is Tudor but only just. You could get away with calling it Plantagenet. Pevsner calls it a splendid building and so it is – when you know its age.

Gainsborough painted the church, the fifth biggest in Suffolk, and made sure of getting Pykenham's Tower in his picture. The church is 15th century Perpendicular with a much earlier tower. The very odd spire looks as if covered in the skin of a sea monster, so silvery-black and scaly does it gleam. Opposite, on the other side of the churchyard, is the Guildhall, lovelier than Lavenham's to my mind, a timber-framed sunset-coloured building.

Timbers and branches

122

Hadleigh High Street and its extension, Benton Street, is a string of marvellous old houses. TVs and videos are for sale in late mediaeval halls with jettied fronts. Some have carved eaves. White brick has never been better used than in some of the Georgian buildings. A former animal feed shop, now an estate agent's, has a 17th century wall painting inside. You used to be able to take a look at it when you went in for a pound of dried cat food.

The visitor can find all about Hadleigh's buildings in Pevsner, who waxes most enthusiastic. He mentions Roman remains of the 3rd century AD found north of the railway line. The line has become a footpath walk, for trains no longer run to Hadleigh which was once one of the termini of the Eastern Union Railway. It is more than 50 years since the trains ceased to carry passengers but in 1933 my predecessors in this house collected from Hadleigh station, where it had been delivered

Brickwork on Pykenham's Tower (opposite)

Hadleigh Guildhall

from London, a pump for raising water from the stream up into the house. The price was £9, a considerable sum in those days.

Soon after John Greenwood married Joanna Lungley of Nussteads, when Mary Tudor was on the throne, Dr Rowland Taylor, the Rector of Hadleigh, was martyred for his intransigent Protestantism. There is an obelisk to him which no one could see and few knew about until the coming of the Hadleigh by-pass. It stands by the hedge on the side of a vast field, facing across the road the shoebox-shaped factories of Hadleigh's no doubt necessary industrial estate.

Taylor passed his last night in the dungeon beneath the Wool Hall in Lavenham, chained to the wall. The curious came to stare at him. He was grateful when they told him he would pass through Hadleigh, where his flock was, on his way to the stake. The burning took place on Aldham Common where the obelisk is, now clearly visible from the new road. Simon Dewes, in 'A Suffolk Childhood', says that a man in the crowd generously despatched him with a cleaver before the flames reached him. But Dewes also seems to have believed that the meeting place of the Hadleigh Conference, its aim the 'Return to Rome', and Taylor's library were one and the same room. If it were true, the irony would be chilling.

The angel in the doorway

The spire of St Mary's, Hadleigh (opposite)

FOUR LIONS AND
FOUR WILD MEN

A font defaced

Moontree (opposite)

It was P. D. James who told me about Covehithe. I asked her to recommend a place on the Suffolk coast for someone not fond of the seaside. She knows far more about our county's coastline than I do or ever shall. I took her advice and was not disappointed.

The tower of St Andrew's can be seen from far out at sea, a dark beacon which points into the sky above the shore north of Southwold and south of Benacre Broad. A little squat building with a thatched roof clings to its side. Only ruins remain to show what a splendid example of English Perpendicular this church was, but once it rivalled Blythburgh for magnificence. Within the ruined walls sheep graze and set up a bleating when visitors come to this serene but melancholy place.

The stairs in the north aisle show that once a great rood screen spanned nave and aisles. Lofty windows, a pair of narrow tall ones that flanked the high altar, indicate that this must have been one of the finest churches in the county. Lambs leap and skip among the remains of the 15th century fabric. The mighty chequered tower rises to a height of 100 feet. There are some stone corbels of royal heads where the vanished nave roof once joined the tower, a few battered little stone angels, and that is almost all apart from the font, now standing inside the church within a church.

It is an octagonal font, made 500 years ago, with four lions and four wild men round the shaft, the winged creatures of the Evangelists with angel minstrels round the bowl. William Dowsing, the iconoclast of the Reformation, who was born at Coddenham and lived at Laxfield, seems to have spared the font in his own village church. Some say because he was christened in it. Elsewhere he was relentless. He defaced the font at Covehithe as well as smashing stained glass, breaking down 'two hundred pictures, one Pope with diverse Cardinals,

Christ and the Virgin Mary, a picture of God the Father'. But it was not his action nor that of Cromwell's agents which reduced the old edifice to its present state. The building was simply too large for the population which never exceeded three hundred souls. The village people themselves pulled it down in 1672 when all but the tower was dismantled and the materials sold.

The ring of five bells, overhauled and re-established, is noted for its lovely tone. There is nothing much between tower and sea. Fields under agriculture and lines of trees distorted by the wind lead down to the low cliffs. The shingle beach is broken by ridges of brown sandstone. The farmer has planted his wheat on one side of the path and his barley on the other up to the cliff edge. Is it familiarity or plain nerve that makes him take his tractor up to the very rim of this eroding coast?

A thin blue mist hangs over the horizon. The beach is brown and a pale brown sea laps it. The only building visible from here is the church tower, a bluish crenellated silhouette. Police notices warn visitors, as if they were in an NCP or shopping arcade, that car thieves operate here. In a huge green field, clean pigs live in the smartest and most hygienic of sties, and the big meadow looks like a camp of mini-Nissen huts for a porcine army.

John Bale, the Protestant controversialist, was born in Covehithe in 1495. He wrote 'Kynge Johan', said to be the first English history play. They called him Bilious Bale because his tongue was so bitter in argument and his satire so virulent. Frequently attacked for his religious views, once imprisoned, he fled to the continent until Elizabeth I came to the throne in 1558. He must throughout his youth have attended St Andrew's in its mediaeval glory and heard its bells ring out over the flat misty land to the sea.

St Andrew's, Covehithe

The encroaching sea
(overleaf)